ALL BETS ARE OFF

ARE OFF

MY JOURNEY OF LOSING 200 POUNDS,
A SHOWDOWN WITH DIABETES, AND
FALLING IN LOVE WITH RUNNING

D1664600

BETSY HARTLEY

CONTENTS

FOREWORD
By Jennifer Viña

You don't easily forget the first time you meet Betsy Hartley. Maybe it's her patent smile. Or the way she confidently stretches out her hand to introduce herself. Her strong grip grabs you, reels you in with a curiosity and intensity that takes you by surprise. She makes eye contact and starts to ask you questions as if she wants to know you. It doesn't matter if you're a college president or working the grocery check out line, when Betsy talks to you, she makes you feel as if you are the only person in the room. Like a warm fire on a crisp autumn night, you're just drawn in.

My dear friend has always been kind, smart, and larger than life. When we first met 12 years ago, her personality was in a much larger body, although that was not the first thing one noticed. As we became friends, to me, her weight was just part of her. I didn't know Bets before type 2 diabetes and a weight problem had overwhelmed her. This was the only version of her I'd ever known.

Ours is the kind of friendship that goes weeks or months without a single word. Suddenly, one of us sends the other a quick message, and two days later we're meeting for lunch.

Through the years, we had not spent a lot of our time together talking about weight or weight loss. Then one day, a year after her mom's passing, we found ourselves in a familiar catch-up session. As we updated each other over burritos and taco salads, she brought up her deepest and most vulnerable challenges. I listened as she opened up her heart to me, pouring out her struggles in the most honest, exposed way. I remember thinking "Me, too, Bets. I feel that too."

She wanted my advice. Advice?! Here I was leaning in to every aspect of her story with my own testimony of fluctuating numbers on the scale, mediocre success, with exercise and exhaustion from feeling lost at where to begin. And she wanted *my* advice?

But I realized she was asking in earnest. So I did what any good friend does: I thought about what she would tell me in this case. I thought about all the things we hear, over and over. The simple, basic formula that we know is tried and true. It isn't hard, but it is hard to maintain day in and day out and often the hardest piece is just getting started.

I told her to grab a napkin. What was her big goal? What would it take? When would she get there? We spelled it out. Pound by pound. Little by little, as the lunch hour faded away, we built her a plan.

There have been some rough patches. It has been emotional and exciting to see her transform from losing the weight to becoming an ultrarunner and redefining her future on her own terms. She is an amazing inspiration. And she's an unshakeable fighter.

The days and weeks have not been easy. Failed friendships, medical missteps, and other moments have tested her. But she decided something big was going to change and she has never lost sight of that compass.

It was too early during that lunch session to know that this would be a moment that would define both of our lives so markedly. Betsy reminds me often of that day and its impact on her life. She doesn't always see or realize how much that day changed my own life.

Like so many of us, I struggle with my own weight, having prioritized motherhood, career, and life's commitments over self-care. Watching Betsy overcome huge obstacles is a constant reminder for me as I look in the mirror, wondering when I'll find the time, the stamina, and the courage to focus on myself. There's irony in being credited with helping a friend when often I can't find the words to encourage myself.

By bravely asking for help, Betsy opened up a world of support for herself. She said what so many of us are thinking, and she has achieved what so many of us yearn for—the confidence and strength to pursue our dreams.

As you read the following pages, you'll learn her story, so deeply personal yet so universally relatable.

Her struggle is my struggle. It might be yours, too. If you allow her, I suspect you'll find a friend to walk beside you. Someone who might have a few tips, or someone who is willing to offer you a napkin so you can start dreaming big.

AUTHOR'S NOTE

This book started as a blog. A blog with about three readers. In the very beginning, it was a way to capture and reflect on what was happening on a journey that was chaotic and complicated and at times unbelievable. It was a public forum and an easy way for me to answer oft-asked questions about losing 200 pounds, exercising while obese, learning to run, and reversing type 2 diabetes. My initial blogs focused solely on those topics, and I was really trying to talk to others who found themselves all alone on the same kind of mind-bogglingly information-scarce journey to a totally new lifestyle. I was not trying to answer the "why" or "how" it happened.

This book attempts to blend all of the blog posts together with some insights and recent learnings about how all the pieces of my story tie together. This book was written because I wanted to tell anyone who finds themselves at 100-plus pounds overweight, with a type 2 diabetes diagnosis, and trying to achieve a goal with the cards stacked against them … *there is hope*. There is a way to fight for your health. It's hard work, and there's no set formula, but there are ways to reverse the path you are on.

Statistics and information on diabetes all come from the American Diabetes Association. I had type 2 diabetes. Where I mention diabetes as it refers to me, it means type 2 diabetes.

All names used are real, legit people in my life. They're the characters I love deeply and I'm happy I get to share these wonderful people with you.

Inconsistencies with weights, dates, or other information are simply author error or a snapshot of real life, because the human body doesn't stay constant.

ALONE ON A MOUNTAIN (AUGUST 2016)

I lost myself on a mountain Friday.

And I found myself.

I found myself in a tent village of 550 trail runners from all over the world beside a pristine alpine lake at Camp Hale, Colorado, two miles above sea level. We had gathered to run 120 miles and climb 20,000 vertical feet in six days. The people who surrounded me understood my desire to run really long distances for fun — mainly because they like doing the same.

Stage Five of the TransRockies Run is hard. A lot of people have struggled with it. I felt strong, as it was the kind of running I like and it included 13 miles of serious power hiking. So I raced my ass off. I ended the day in 35th place for women for the stage. I had never had a solid result like that before. That in itself would be justification for a few tears of joy. But another emotional tidal wave washed over me during and after the stage.

Around Checkpoint Two, the second aid station on the course, I had what I can only describe as a breakthrough. It slammed me in the chest and in the brain, and I'm still trying to figure out exactly what in the hell happened. I ran through the checkpoint, grabbing a slice of watermelon and a small cup of Coke, stuffed energy gels in my pack, refilled my water, and barreled out of the station.

I was running on a ridgeline above Vail. I looked left and right, and all I could see was jaw-dropping scenery, mountains and trees and puffy white clouds in a blindingly blue sky. It took my breath away, thinking about the beauty that I could run in and was seeing up close. This is my life, I thought. I'm running for six whole days. In the Rocky Mountains.

This is my *life*!

I thought about my friends who had traveled with me from Oregon, who were all strong and fast runners and would be waiting for me in camp. I thought about new friends I had already made on this trip, people who I strongly suspected would become lifelong friends.

I'm running. I'm hiking. I'm healthy.

Then the shovel hit me in the face.

I am a trail runner.

I AM NO LONGER A 400-POUND WOMAN.

I had been waiting for the day when I would no longer instantly pull up the image of my former self. I had always been the heavy girl. I still saw myself that way. I was still periodically startled when I did not recognize my own reflection. I think I'd been waiting to see a certain number on the scale, or a certain size on the label of the pants I was buying. Truth be told, I had no clue what I was really waiting for to fully understand that obesity was no longer my life or my identity.

In the same vein, I've never called myself "a runner." And that pisses off Spencer, my running coach and business partner, to no end. I run and workout and train and race, but have refused to see myself as a runner simply because I don't look like a typical runner. Call it imposter syndrome.

Today, on that exposed ridge above Vail, with no one around, I ran. On the dirt. Bawling. Gasping for breath, not just because of the 12,000-foot altitude, but because I was totally overwhelmed with happiness and understanding and acceptance. Suddenly understanding that being a runner isn't how you look, it's what you do. The identity is simply yours to own if you want it.

I kept running and the tears just kept running as well. I got to Checkpoint Three and saw my friend Michael "Fitzy" Fitzpatrick, a Canadian ultrarunner who was volunteering at TransRockies. He's the sort of guy who wears outlandish costumes while ringing cowbells, who shouts loud, energetic encouragement at every single runner, at every stage of the race. I learned on day one of this event that he cheers for everyone. Every single last one of us. Even us back-of-the-packers.

Fitzy, Hope Pass, Colorado, TransRockies 2016.

I ran up to him and barreled into him for a sweaty hug. I'm sure my face was streaked with tears when I almost knocked him over, cowbells clanging. I said in a single breath, "Fitzy! I'm tired and I want to be done running, but I've had the best running day so far! Please put on your coach's hat and tell me to run the five miles down the hill as hard as I can!" Fitzy said, "Run! Go! You can do this! I'm proud of you!" I grabbed watermelon and Coke, and took off again. I remembered how Spencer had taught me to descend hills on legs that are tired. I was moving fast and strong and confident on the straight downhill stretches. I could feel all the training I'd been doing over the past year kicking in and taking over.

About halfway down that hill, I was passed by Brett, a runner and triathlete from Chicago. I had shared parts of the trail with him briefly each day. He was usually way ahead of me by the halfway mark, and I didn't see much of him until dinner. Today we were down to the last five kilometers before he slipped past. "Come on, Betsy!" he yelled with a huge grin on his face, "Run!" And I thought, here's a guy who sees me as a runner. Not a fat girl. Just a runner. And that shovel of realization hit me again.

Approaching the finish line, I could hear Spencer's voice amongst the other runners all gathered around the finish line cheering on all our fellow runners. He would tell me later he was surprised at how fast I had run that segment. Hell yes. I was too! If there was one person in this world who understood the complicated package of my fat-girl psyche, my refusal to identify and claim my rights as a runner, knew how hard I trained for a full year to be ready for this multi-day stage race, it was Spencer Newell. I ran as fast as I could to the finish line and then found him. As I choked back those freaking tears, I told Spencer with no preamble, "I'm not that 400-pound woman anymore. I'm a trail runner. I left the fat girl on the mountain." His reply was, "About time."

Later in the day, I sat in front of Spencer's tent for our daily coaching debrief. We would use this time to review the day's run and discuss our approach, strategy, and plans for the next stage. This debrief, however, was hijacked by my emotional distress. I was raw. I was trying to process this and not lose the wildly unfamiliar and desperately welcomed feeling of "ditching the fat girl." He kept telling me to write it all down. I kept telling him that I had no fucking clue what had happened, but I knew that it was undeniably a life-altering moment.

And it was.

Words can't do this moment justice. They can't. This was about a change of heart.

The shift has been a long time coming. It's about letting go of the familiar steel anchor that held me back even as it kept me comfortable. It's scary as hell. I feel totally and utterly confused as I try to understand what happened on that mountain. I feel grateful. I feel stunned. Perhaps I'll never entirely know what it was, or be able to explain it.

When I woke up that morning, I believed that I could run, work hard, give 100 percent effort, and still be nothing more than a formerly 400-pound woman who took up trail running as a hobby to lose weight. I am about to crawl into my tent to go to bed, a trail runner. I found running, and then running saved my life—running, and the people in the trail-running community. I am a trail runner who can lay down a great personal effort because I've been trained, and I've paid attention, and I've worked hard. It's not a payment for past sins. I am a trail runner.

Tomorrow is Stage Six. I'm going to fight like hell, run my ass off, and savor every single step of the journey. I'm going to celebrate finding myself in the Rockies.

1 CHAPTER ONE
NAMING THE ELEPHANT IN THE ROOM

I lost over 200 pounds, reversed type 2 diabetes, and learned to run. That's me in a nutshell. To say that everything in my life has changed is an understatement.

When I started this process, I had no real idea where it was going to lead me. None. How could I? I started out blindly and took things one step at a time. There weren't a ton of people who, at least publicly, talked about reversing diabetes and losing triple-digits weight. So it would be fair to say I was winging it. A whole lot of what I was doing was just blindly falling forward and hoping I was stumbling in roughly the right direction.

So, how the hell did I get to be 400 pounds? If anyone pointedly asked me that question, I would shrug and blame diabetes and genetics and laziness. And I would creatively avoid directly addressing the topic for lack of any more depth to my answers. And that should have been a big, fat hint.

The truth is harder and more complicated to unravel. Finding that truth is something that happened along the way. When I started writing this book, it was going to be neat and tidy—tell everyone how I lost weight and reversed diabetes, and throw in that I learned to run, and (spoiler alert!) how I ran a 100-miler. Be done. Well, as you'd guess, it's not that simple. Not by a long shot. By not talking about how I got to be 400 pounds, I would miss the chance to connect with people about how my life reached dire straits before I turned it all around. And when I started writing my blog and even later, this book, it wasn't entirely clear to me. It's becoming much clearer with each passing day.

Sometimes the middle of the story is where everything starts to make sense. At least it's worked that way for me.

Unraveling the question of how I got to be 400 pounds began when Spencer Newell, my running coach, friend, and business partner, asked me in the spring of 2017 to write a short list about *why I run*. I'd been running for about four years at that point and told everyone who would listen just how much I loved running. So I thought for a few days and wrote a list that was complete with heart-shaped bullets to start off each statement. It was rainbows, unicorns, and cupcakes with sprinkles. I believed what I had written to be the truth. I printed it out and put it on the fridge. It was things like "I love being known as a runner," "I love belonging to the running community," and "I love being one with nature." After carefully reading my list, Spencer not-too-gently told me he thought my list was crap. That might be a direct quote. Or he might have said, "This is bullshit and doesn't come close to why you really run."

I was feeling pretty squished. I mean, didn't *I* know why *I* loved running? What the hell? Yet there was something in his unamused, blunt tone that made me stop and really consider his feedback. We had worked together long enough, and had banked some serious trust and respect for each other. I *had* to appreciate that he'd told me a truth as he saw it. There were a whole lot of mental and emotional gymnastics that consumed the next two years after I wrote that list. Deep down I knew Spencer was right. I knew something hidden was stirring and trying to surface. I knew he was pushing me to get honest with myself. I also knew it wasn't just going to be about running.

I look back and realize it was a moment that opened a brand-new door that I would have to walk through. Tip of the iceberg. Mouth of the lion. Pick your scary-ass analogy for jumping off the edge of the known toward the unknown — all to figure out what makes you *you* — I was there.

I stood at the edge for a while, trying to decide if I even wanted to do the work to figure this all out. I was confused by it all. I mean, I thought I had *done* the work. I thought when I started this journey more than eight years ago, that when I reversed diabetes or hit a number on the scale, I would have arrived. I'd be *done*. I simply had no idea of the unfinished work that would be exposed when I lost the weight. Life, as she does sometimes, conspired to nudge me off the edge. Here's the timeline from the last two years while I was trying to process *why I run:*

- "Why I Run" list declared "crap" in the spring of 2017

- Acute binge-eating episode in the fall of 2017

- Significant knee injury in the winter of 2018

- Started therapy and willingly walked off that scary-ass edge into self-discovery in the summer of 2018

None of these events seemed genuinely related at the time, yet all are deeply melded and blended in the rearview mirror. It all started with my inability to honestly answer the simple question: *Why do you run?* Working with a therapist, I have been learning what is broken, how to heal and move forward, and how to prevent the past from keeping me in a stranglehold. I've been working to unearth and strengthen my self-confidence. And I now have some solid coping skills to help me along.

Why do I eat to manage my emotions? Where the hell did I get conditioned to avoid and hide from certain emotions, anyway? What happened as I was growing up to mess me up so completely that I don't even like myself most days? Why did I develop a warped set of tools to "survive" life? It's a fucking complicated path, I can tell you that much.

So how did I get to be 400 pounds?

My story involves being bullied and shamed by those closest to me, by friends, family members, teachers. Unkind and repetitive messages and experiences that wore and tore down my self-worth, made me question if I was lovable or desirable or worthy. Food became my reliable solace and comfort in that pain and confusion. I was told in many ways that being fat was not okay. I could never be a valued professional. No one would ever be attracted to me. I would never have kids. I would have to work a fuck-ton harder than anyone else to make anything out of my life. I got that message loud and clear, and I ate to dull the shame and pain of it all.

So you probably want to know what bullying and shaming looked like in my life.

- Opening my annual Christmas gift from an extended family member that was always at least two sizes too small, letting me know what size they thought I should be, instead of accepting the size I was.

- Being called fat and ugly to my face.

- Watching my mom, who was overweight and wheelchair bound for 40 plus years, be dismissed as weak and treated differently in countless ways.

- Being asked to be in a wedding party because my size would make the already thin bride look even smaller.

- Having the boy at the school dance look me up and down carefully when I asked him if he would like to dance and say, "Uh, yeah ... but not with you."

- Having a relative pinch my belly-fat roll as I reached for a holiday cookie and say, "Don't you think you've had enough, young lady?"

- Enduring a fifth grade teacher who called me "Beefy Betsy," isolated my desk from others so they had "room," and encouraged my classmates to pick me first for dodgeball because I was a "big, fat, and easy target."

- Hearing family friends make comments about how I was a beautiful girl, but it was a shame I was too fat for anyone to date.

- Soaking in the words of the endless stream of doctors who gave abrupt or incomplete care, coupled with unsolicited weight-loss advice, when I was seeing them for totally unrelated issues.

- Experiencing the eye rolls and groans from moviegoers, airplane passengers, and classmates if I (and my bulk) sat next to them.

Can I stop now? Get the idea?

I had a childhood filled with love, happy memories, and good times. Yet I grew up understanding that being fat was not okay. I understood that to mean *I* was not okay. I absorbed it each time it was reinforced. Accepted it. Became it.

I always had a smile on my face. I always tried to embrace the positive. I believe that most of the people in my life would tell you I am a positive, happy and optimistic person. And I am. Yet, inside... I was hiding humiliation and shame. For decades. I was trying with everything in me to compensate for my fat life in the only way I knew how: deflection and overt, fake happiness. I was busy living a life that was built around apologizing for who I was. And food was my stalwart companion in the misery. Food never judged, never left me feeling alone. Eating was always a happy moment, or a moment of relief, no matter what was going on around me. Food was the perfect accompaniment to stuff down unpalatable emotions, to quiet the fear of confrontation and dull the sharp pain of shame. I developed binge eating disorder (BED) as a coping mechanism to deal with the feelings I couldn't manage in other healthier ways. Food helped me feel loved, like I belonged, and like I was not alone. I gave that power to food.

That is how I got from being 400 pounds, grappling with diabetes, to trying to unravel *why in the hell I run* at 50 years old and already eight years in on my lifestyle change. I said it was a complicated path. Let's take a walk back to the beginning of this journey.

"You are Very Sick"

I first heard the word "prediabetic" when I was 28 years old, in 1996. I remember thinking that "pre" meant I had time. I really wish I could have understood what was coming. The doctors didn't seem concerned, so why should I worry about it? They said, "This means you could develop diabetes at some point. We'll keep an eye on things. We want you to eat better and lose some weight." Knowing what I know now, I wish they had said, "You have one last chance to avoid a devastating disease. Listen up! This is in your hands, and you are running out of time to stop it!"

As much as I would love to blame anyone but myself, I know I wasn't ready to listen. I wasn't ready to hear it. I was playing ostrich. If I buried my head in the sand, maybe this would all just go away. Diabetes would mean I had to change what, when, and how I ate. This was going to get messy and scary and not fun. Life was going to suck. If I was only prediabetic, I could postpone dealing with it. Right? I was flirting with a deadline disease. My messed-up relationship with food had me in a complete chokehold. Rather than being paralyzed by the facts, I was totally refusing to accept them. I was paralyzed by my denial.

Sometime in 2000, a few pivotal things happened in roughly the same time frame. I was forced to confront reality. I had a foot wound that would not heal, so my general doc sent me to a wound specialist. The specialist suggested trying to heal it with one more round of antibiotics before we would have to talk about cutting out the infected area. I heard the words "partial amputation" and about passed out. He said it was because my blood sugars were not well controlled, so I was not healing well.

At about the same time, I went to see my gynecologist. She was reviewing my lab reports and asked me what medications I was taking for diabetes. "None," I told her, "I'm only prediabetic." "No, you are full-blown type 2 diabetic," she said slowly, obviously stunned I was hearing this for the first time. "There's no more of this 'pre' crap. You are very sick." She made me an appointment with a diabetes specialist for the very next day. Being an ostrich had not worked. Not for a moment.

I was not type 1 diabetic. Type 1 is an autoimmune disease. I was type 2 diabetic, which is largely acknowledged as a dietary disease. Genes load the gun, for sure, but most of us with type 2 diabetes have fired the trigger on ourselves through poor food choices, inactivity, stress, and often poor sleep driving us to become overweight (especially belly fat). We ultimately develop prediabetes and then diabetes.

Two blood tests confirmed that I was type 2 diabetic. The hemoglobin A1c (Hgb A1c) blood test measured how well I managed my blood glucose over a three-month period, and a fasting blood-sugar test that was essentially a real-time reading. Both were way too high. Instead of the 4.8 to 5.7 range, where it belonged, my A1c was 11.2. My fasting blood sugar should have been between 80 and 120. Mine was 342. I had symptoms, serious symptoms, that I was ignoring. I blamed them on my obesity, but I didn't realize they were also tied to my diabetes. Over the years, I had adapted and accepted my reduced quality of life as part of being grossly overweight.

What were my symptoms?

Sores and blisters would not heal. Common colds would last for weeks. Small skin wounds or cuts in my mouth would take forever to heal.

I could not sleep enough. I was barely getting through the day. I was not just sleepy, I was groggy and foggy all the time. Although I slept for 10 to 12 hours a day, I fell asleep in meetings, while driving my car, and on phone calls. It was suggested I had sleep apnea, common in type 2 diabetic and obese patients, but I was never formally diagnosed. I slept 15 to 18 hours a day on weekends.

I could not get enough to eat. I could eat until I was stuffed, physically over-full, and still feel hungry. When you suffer from type 2 diabetes, your body just can't use its fuel efficiently. It was like putting diesel in a gas engine. I could consume 5,000 calories a day and still be hungry.

Sugar. I wanted sugar.

Shots and Needles

The first time I visited a doctor who specialized in treating diabetes, he literally gave me a bag with a vial of insulin and a handful of syringes in it. Then he did an about-face pivot and walked out the door. I was scared to death. Being told I was full-blown diabetic was scary enough; now I was going to be on insulin. I was given no instructions on how to give myself a shot. It was all too much. The doctor did tell me the shots had to be administered in a very specific way, within an eight-inch radius of my belly button. Did I understand what he was telling me? I numbly nodded yes. I tend to do that when I am totally intimidated or totally lost. I sat there, dazed and confused, and started to cry.

Nurse Mae walked into the room. "I don't know how to give myself a shot," I wailed. "And I have to." Mae calmly talked me through the process. "We'll figure this out together," she reassured me. She explained each thing in my bag and how it was used. She told me to get a sharps container and alcohol pads. She helped me visualize how to give myself a shot. I dried the tears and, after a while, I walked out. I knew that I had no choice. I just had to learn.

I got home and put everything on the counter. I fished around for what I needed and eventually drew the meds into the syringe. Then I stood there, thumb on the plunger, needle pointed at my belly … I had to do this. There was no Nurse Mae here. So I started "dancing." I don't know what else to call it. I began to chase myself around the kitchen. I would try to bring the syringe in close, then I would back away from myself. I have no other explanation. Had anyone been watching, I am sure it would have looked totally ridiculous.

And then I stood still, with the needle poised, just willing myself to administer the damned shot. I could not do it. I cried some more. I stomped my feet. I threw the syringe. I took a deep breath. I cursed fluently and creatively.

Finally, I retrieved the syringe and checked to make sure it was all in one piece and that the right amount of insulin was still in it.

Okay.

So maybe if I metaphorically took a "running jump?" What if I stopped thinking about it so much, and just jumped in with both feet? That's how people conquer things they are afraid of, right? They just do it. So I grabbed the syringe with both hands, stood there for a moment, and finally got up the nerve to ... stab myself in the gut. *Hard.* It must have been like the dagger scene from *Romeo and Juliet.* I used enough force that I knocked the wind out of myself. I wound up sporting a faint, softball-sized bruise on my belly, one that looked remarkably like my fist. But I got it done! Those needles are fine-gauge and short. You can barely feel them. Honestly! There were several times over the years when I gave myself a shot and had to look down and check to make sure the needle had actually pierced my belly.

That first time I had to give myself a shot? It was one of the hardest things I'd ever had to do. I felt only pure fear. But I got it done. Nike has it right. I just did it.

What's the Difference?

Type 1 and type 2 diabetes are vastly different.

Type 1 diabetes is an autoimmune disease. The body attacks and kills the insulin-producing beta cells that are made in the pancreas. Sometimes type 1 is called "juvenile diabetes." And it's deadly without modern medicine. There is no cure. Insulin is not a cure. It's simply a medicine that keeps type 1 diabetics alive, hopefully, until a cure is found. Eating or not eating sugar, sweets, and carbohydrates are a part of their own personal care routine to balance blood glucose and insulin, minute by minute. While diet changes don't solve the fact that people with type 1 diabetes have an autoimmune disease and their pancreas doesn't work, low sugar diets tend to lead to more stable, normal blood sugars and less reliance on high insulin doses which result in highs and lows.

Type 2 diabetes is a metabolic disorder and is the most common form of the disease. It used to be commonly referred to as "adult-onset" diabetes but sadly, with childhood obesity on the rise, we now see it in children too, thus the name change. Type 2 diabetics produce increasing levels of insulin that the body can't use very well. With high insulin levels, the pancreas produces and stores more sugar as fat, leading to a vicious cycle of increased hunger, more sugar consumption, and more fat. Type 2 diabetes is largely acknowledged as a lifestyle disease. In my case, years of poor food choices and lack of activity propelled me into type 2 diabetes. Genetics, pancreatic injury, and other illness can also play a role in its development and severity.

Although my body makes plenty of insulin, through years of abuse I had messed up the receptors that recognize insulin and know how to use it. Think about trying to use a baseball glove to catch a soccer ball. It just doesn't work very well. It was my own damn doing.

The protocol for managing type 2 diabetes is usually in this order of intervention: Lifestyle changes (food and activity), oral medications, and injectable insulin. Diet and exercise are scientifically proven, critical components in the successful management of diabetes.

Here are some statistics, published by the American Diabetes Association, to help put this monster (and growing) disease into perspective:

- 1.5 million Americans are diagnosed with diabetes each year

- 1.25 million are type 1 diabetics

- 30.3 million are type 2 diabetics

- 9.4 percent of the population has diabetes

- Diabetes is the seventh leading cause of death

- The annual cost of caring for those with diabetes is $327 billion

- One in four health care dollars is spent caring for those with diabetes

For more information on the costs and social ramifications of diabetes, check out http://www.diabetes.org.

The numbers are climbing fast in the wrong direction. While I'm not sure if I know the exact words we should be using to discuss the issue, I keep hearing my doctors and health care folks use words like "epidemic," "staggering," and "out of control," and even "global pandemic." Given what I am learning about both forms of diabetes, the people afflicted, and the skyrocketing costs for care, those words seem sadly apt. One of my missions in life is to work to help reverse these trends.

Boiling A Frog

When my sister, Deb, got married in 2003, I was 5-foot-7 and weighed 399 pounds. It might have been more, but the numbers on our scale didn't even go that high. I was a full-blown, insulin-dependent type 2 diabetic. I gave myself three shots a day and took a fistful of prescription medications. Morbidly obese, I had a serious aversion to sweating. I wore size 26/28 (4X). I had high blood pressure and super-sketchy cholesterol numbers. I had fatty liver disease. I had chronic open sores on my feet that wouldn't heal for months on end. I needed an extender for the seatbelt on an airplane. There was no way I could sit in a folding chair without its legs collapsing. I was often asked if I were pregnant.

One of the few pictures I have at 400-pounds is from my sister's wedding. When you weigh this much, you tend to be camera shy.

I was eating between 4,000 and 5,000 calories a day. I had a seriously screwed up relationship with food that had controlled me for my entire life. I thought about food from the time I woke up until I went to bed. I was addicted to food and the comfort it gave. I would make or change plans based on food. My happiest moments were centered on food. It owned me. I was slowly and surely killing myself with poor food choices and an utter lack of any kind of physical activity. I'd avoided sweat, ironically, with freaking Olympic gold-medal effort. I was overweight most of my life, with only fleeting diet success that involved starvation and no way to stay that hungry and momentarily thin.

My mom was overweight, mostly from the autoimmune drugs used to ease the pain of her rheumatoid arthritis (RA). She'd been diagnosed with RA in her early thirties when my sister and I were still in grade school. By the time I was in my thirties, my mom was having hip and knee joints replaced on a regular basis and relied increasingly on a wheelchair because of her ankles degenerating. In the years leading up to her death, she was entirely wheelchair dependent. My dad, on the other hand, was trim and active. Hell, at 75 he can *still* stand flat-footed and put the palms of his hands flat on the ground. He single-handedly runs a 200-acre family hazelnut farm. My sister Deb struggled with her weight in middle school, but by high school, she'd changed her habits and was a standout on her high school basketball team and was the only girl on her small-school men's baseball team. She still maintains a stable weight with some intentional effort.

Being obese, I often struggled with feeling out of place and like I didn't belong. I was a master at using food and my extroverted personality and big-ass smile and self-deprecating comments to mask my internal misery from the rest of the world. My favorite "weapon" to handle emotional discomfort? Food. A shit-ton of food. Years of food. So it is no real mystery that after years and years of poor food choices and no activity, diabetes found me. And it tackled me to the ground.

Type 2 diabetes could be managed with drugs. Google said so. And how serious was it, really? Plenty of people lived long lives with it. There were worse things than giving myself shots. I had a job I loved, young nephews I adored, and wonderful family and friends. I had convinced myself that my life was good, that I could manage "a few" health problems, and that type 2 diabetes was not that big of a deal. My denial game was strong for a very long time.

Prior to the diabetic diagnosis, I would diet from time to time. Whatever easy, magic, or secret diet was popular, I climbed aboard the wagon. I didn't really give any of them a chance or perhaps now is the time to speak a truth: "diets" are not designed to help you succeed when what you need is a shift in your entire lifestyle. And some of them rely on your failure to ensure repeat business. Think about it.

Anyway, I tried all the popular ones you can name. Fen-phen. Nutrisystem. Weight Watchers. Alli. Medifast. South Beach. Atkins. Jenny Craig. Cabbage soup. At one point I even tried to order a tapeworm via a mail order ad in a magazine (I really wish I was kidding…). As soon as I was starving, when I couldn't take the hunger anymore, the diet failed. I'd go right back to ignoring my obesity, hoping the weight would fall off as soon as the right diet came along.

Becoming grossly overweight is best told with the analogy of how you boil a frog. If you first boil a pot of water, then throw a frog in, it will immediately hop back out to safety. But if you place that same frog in a pot of cold water and turn up the heat gradually, you will wind up with perfectly boiled frog's legs. The frog doesn't realize what's happening, doesn't feel a need to jump to safety, and accepts each passing moment as a new reality. It eventually kills him.

I got to be 399 pounds because I slowly adapted to my increasing bulk. It never alarmed me in the day-to-day. I just woke up one day and realized I weighed nearly 400 pounds. It was killing me. By the time I hit my forties, I had frankly given up hope of ever losing weight. I was flirting nonstop with apathy. I knew I weighed a ridiculous amount. I was just destined to be fat and lonely and give into the eventual ravages of diabetes. To reverse this train wreck would take serious, unbearably hard work—work I could never, ever stop doing.

An Uneasy Truce

For at least three years before my diagnosis, any outside observer could tell something was seriously wrong with me. I had decided my symptoms were the price I paid for obesity. I simply wasn't ready to fight; I didn't want to make changes. As crappy as things were, I had grown to understand and be comfortable with those things. I was in bad physical shape, yet I was willing to stay there because I was utterly overwhelmed by the thought of what it would take to make things different. You accept and allow what you think you are worth.

Being diagnosed as a full-blown diabetic threw everything I knew and loved out the nearest window, just as I had feared it would. I heard the diagnosis and spent four months grieving. I was put on meds for depression. I totally cut myself off from friends and the outside world. I threw an epic pity party, and I was the only guest. Denial. Bargaining. Depression. Acceptance. I was moving randomly through the stages of grief in my own nonsensical order. I had been in deep denial. I had bargained to no avail. I was depressed. Diabetes and I had settled into an early, uneasy truce — a truce that would last for about 10 years.

Emotions battled it out daily. My first six to 12 months as a diabetic were confused and intense. I had a lot to learn, a lot to change. I was not a fun person to be around. The meds started working pretty quickly. They were clearing my brain of the cloudiness that comes with high and sustained glucose levels. I slowly began to see and understand what had happened to me — what I had let happen. I had not stopped the disease when I had the chance. Now I would have to manage it. I couldn't rewrite history, but I could sure as hell write a new ending. I held the pen, in this case the pen needle.

I eventually accepted the idea that I had choices to make:

- I could survive ... or I could thrive

- I could stay ignorant and let the doctors tell me what to do ... or I could learn about the disease and how to manage it

- I could accept that this disease owned me ... or I could fight for my life

Thrive, learn, and fight.

I immediately made diet adjustments when I was diagnosed. Damn, did I hate the changes, but I was too scared not to change. Every single bite of food had to be considered. It was a whole new level of mental fatigue, laced liberally with fear. About four to six weeks in, with the help of meds, I started to feel better. I was less sleepy, less ravenously hungry, and more clearheaded. The results of my effort at eating better began to show in my daily glucose tests. Watching those glucose numbers drop into a more normal daily range was an incentive to keep going with my new eating habits.

As I worked to initially lose weight, get used to the medicine, and establish new eating habits, I experienced highs and lows in my blood sugar that had to be adjusted. Dietary adjustments sometimes threw my entire daily plan out the window. It could be intensely frustrating and confusing. Going back to my old ways and just letting diabetes win was a seriously appealing idea on more than a few occasions. Several times my dad told me, "Get this as right as you can, as often as you can. You'll make progress. Refocus on the very next step you need to take in order to reach your bigger goal. You are doing all the right things. Your body just has to figure out how to work with you now that you are working to get healthy."

The Learning Curve

Life as a diabetic, if you are actively trying to manage the disease, takes serious and relentless work.

I had to learn to count carbohydrates and not eat too many over the course of a day. All carbs in reality have some impact, even the naturally occurring ones. I really started by simply trying to remove overt sugar. Carbs are my favorite, especially the highly processed and packaged carbs, so this was seriously unpleasant work for a very long time. I had lots of temper tantrums on this nasty little learning curve.

I had to learn to stick my finger each morning for a glucose reading. I tried not to bleed all over my clothes or leave my counter looking like a crime scene. I had to manage my medicines, needles, and sharps containers. I was taking seven oral medications and three shots a day. There were lots of bruises and bent needles as I tried to figure out how to stab myself, cursing, in the stomach. I had to manage the side effects from medications. The warning label on one medicine read, "May cause severe gastric distress," and it did. It was an issue every single day. I did not want witnesses. I had to manage type 2 diabetes when I was sick—which meant I was dealing with questionable judgment from a foggy brain, rampaging and nonsensical numbers, dehydration, and drug adjustments.

I began to learn about being physically active. I started small. I took the stairs. I parked my car further away. I drank more water, so I had to get up from my desk to pee more often.

I began to cautiously acknowledge my messed-up relationship with food. I learned to read and understand nutrition labels, and that serving sizes mattered. I learned to track food and count calories. All the food. All the calories. There could be no hiding or lying or cheating or excuses. That was the hardest thing to learn. This would become a lesson I would have to relearn many times. I could lie to myself all I wanted, make any excuse I wanted, but my blood work would eventually rat me out and reveal whether I was doing the necessary work. I had been eating a lot of food, all the wrong kinds of food, for all the wrong reasons—wrong for diabetes and wrong for life.

Being honest about what I was eating and why I was eating was humbling and brutal. There was much learning and changing and scares. I hit stumbling blocks, bad attitudes, and plateaus. I had bad numbers and crappy weeks and major setbacks. Giving up was not an option, even on the worst of days. Even a small amount of progress was still progress. I had to keep reminding myself of that fact.

Thrive, learn, and fight. I had promised myself I was going to live by those words.

I'd forged a solid coexistence with diabetes. We got along quite well for about a decade. I worked to get my numbers stable. I worked to lose weight. I worked on building a better relationship with food. With luck, all of these changes would prevent kidney failure, going blind, or having small chunks of my extremities amputated from nerve damage. My doctor was happy that I was holding my own. It was good enough for a long time. And then one day, "good enough" was no longer good enough. Coexisting and comfortable were no longer working. I began to feel restless and eager and brave. I finally recognized what was emerging: a feeling of being done with it. I was done with diabetes. Done with shots. Done with being fat. Done with accepting that this was going to be the story of my life. I wasn't angry. I wasn't depressed. It was just that "good enough" was not enough anymore. And it never would be again. I was resolute and determined. I wanted to *live*. Diabetes and I were headed for a showdown.

May 2001, about six months prior to me waking up and deciding I wanted to change my life. I'm close to 300 pounds in this picture.

Mom and me. Oregon Coast about two years before her death.

Grieving

My world stopped spinning on March 10, 2010, just after nine in the morning, when my mom died.

It was six days after her 66th birthday.

For months we had been fighting all-out to save her. She had fallen victim to methicillin-resistant staphylococcus aureus (MRSA), a massive, drug-resistant staph infection. This systemic "superbug" could not be controlled by any drugs available in the United States, not even experimental combinations. My mom's immune system had been seriously compromised since she was diagnosed with rheumatoid arthritis (RA) at age 32. Long-term complications of RA were diabetes and kidney failure. She was in the early stages of renal failure when MRSA took hold. She was a desperately difficult case for doctors at Oregon Health Sciences University (OHSU). We were routinely told how dire and complicated things were. And eventually the infection and its complications overwhelmed her body.

I grieved. For more than a year, I was secluded, closed off, and wounded. Hell, I'm still grieving, more than nine years later. My mom was one of my best friends. She shouldn't have died. But her health was so complicated and compromised that her body couldn't help her fight the infection.

After she died, I began to concede a few things in my own life.

Four months prior to her death, at about 380-ish pounds, I had bulged two discs in my lower back when I tripped and fell. The doctor told me the weight I carried in my belly had likely created its own inertia and pulled my vertebrae apart, that the fall alone shouldn't have done it. I was drugged into oblivion for pain management, and crippled to the point that I couldn't bend over my mom's hospital bed to kiss her cheek as she was dying. I will never get over that. I'm not even going to try. Being fat had finally caught up with me. This was the first time I ever remember feeling remorse and disgust at having let myself get so fat and unhealthy. And abject pity for myself because the only other person in the world that would understand any of it was now dead.

At age 42, when my mom died, I was a candidate for a back surgery related to my weight. I was still taking three insulin shots a day along with six or seven other meds. I was being encouraged by my doctor to consider bariatric surgery. I was dependent upon a lot of doctors to keep me as healthy as I believed I was. Yet, as I observed hospital activity during our family time at OHSU, I realized that a good long-term strategy for survival is not to rely on nonstop health care or hospitals. It took about sixteen months for me to piece all this together and decide it was time to act.

Grieving changes a person fundamentally. It tears you to shreds and scars you. You feel as if your heart is bleeding. You are in a blinding mental fog. Yet, oddly, it makes you stronger than you ever thought possible. Suddenly, you are fiercely protective of loved ones and friends. Protecting others becomes the only emotional outlet for the shit storm in your mind and heart. Grief makes you so weak and vulnerable that you sit passively, even in public, with tears streaming down your face because you don't even have the energy to sob. If you've grieved, you know what I'm talking about. You have your own version for what it does to your life, your mind, your heart.

As the days wore on after my mom's passing, the fog began to lift. I began to realize that my mom would be so, so disappointed if I kept living my life as a zombie with one foot willingly in the grave. What kind of tribute to her would that be? She was an incredible, warm-hearted soul who loved life and cherished people until the very end. She enjoyed every moment she was given even in the worst parts of her pain and disease. My sister and I have talked about how we knew our mom as having crippling RA for 30 plus years, and yet we never heard her complain about pain, restrictions, or being in a wheelchair. Ever. She never complained. She appreciated each day as it came. I wanted to do the same — to live a full life, not a half-life of adapting and just getting by. I began to understand that the biggest tribute I could possibly pay to my mom was to choose to live life fully, to love people and enjoy each moment I was given. Things had to change.

Eating an Elephant

How do you eat an elephant? One bite at a time.

I love this truism. It's a fabulous reminder that to accomplish fantastically big things, you simply break them down into a bunch of little pieces. That is how you clean your house. Plan a big event. Earn a college degree. And it's exactly how you would go about eating an elephant.

Triple-digit weight loss was staring me in the face. I was increasingly desperate to reverse a disease that had me in a stranglehold for more than ten years. I had to think small and start small. The big picture would quickly overwhelm me into submission before I even got started.

I remember the intense anxiety and fledgling bravado I felt when I finally knew I was going to lose more than 200 pounds and tackle diabetes. I was desperately tired of being fat. I wanted *off* insulin. And I knew — I had been told multiple times, and I had dug up the research — that the odds were overwhelmingly against me being successful with either endeavor. A freaking elephant was charging straight toward me. I remember thinking panicky, repetitive, self-defeating thoughts when I was trying to make the mental leap to start fighting for my life. Here's the dialogue that was running through my brain:

- No way in hell is this actually going to happen, but I have to start. Diabetes will kill me if I don't. These are my choices. Damn. My choices suck!

- Even when I was born, I don't think I weighed under 175 pounds. (Sorry, mom.) That's my "goal weight?!"

- I have to lose more pounds than what most people ever even weigh!

- It will take years to see progress.

- I have to change everything: Every. Single. Thing.

- What if I can't beat diabetes? What if I have done too much damage to my body?

- Is it true that once you go on injectable insulin, you're screwed? I mean, is it all over? Can I never lose any weight?

- Do I know anyone who has lost a huge amount of weight and kept it off? Anyone?

- Do I know anyone who has reversed type 2 diabetes? (I hear crickets.)

- No one understands how hard this is going to be. No one. Holy crap. I am alone.

- Food. Oh, no. Food. Why does this have to involve food?

- Exercise? Are you freaking kidding me? Wear spandex in front of people? No way! That alone will kill me!

- Where do I even begin? (Panic, tears, shame).

- Once I get started, I can never, ever stop. This is for the rest of my life.

Repeat cycle. Reinforce negative thinking. Talk yourself out of taking action, because you can't really do this ...

And then I went to lunch with my friend Jennifer Viña in late spring of 2011. Jennifer and I worked together at Oregon State University. We started around the same time, in different areas of work, but clicked immediately. She's a wicked smart woman, talented writer, and loyal friend. We can go weeks without talking and then simply pick right back up where we were. She's kind and I had countless examples of how generously non-judgmental she was.

I was at the point where my goals of mega weight loss, abolishing diabetes, and getting healthy were becoming stronger than my fears. My desire to live was finally eclipsing my fear of dying! I verbally vomited all over Jennifer. In an unorganized, frantic, tear-filled session, I confided in her what I really wanted to do. I was finally saying this out loud to another person. She listened to it all.

Then she made me write everything down. How much I weighed. What I wanted to lose. How long it would take. Precise dates. What would happen if I lost one pound a week? There were no fears allowed. No hedging. Only unwavering encouragement. She gently, but pointedly, forced me to think about what I wanted and exactly how to get there. She showed me how to eat the elephant.

I left with my plan written on a napkin ... and a huge life gift. She convinced me that I could do it. I could do anything. I just had to break it down. This was the first time I felt that it might all be possible. My confidence would come and go many, many times; it still does, to be honest. This first hint of confidence was amazing! "You just have to start. Then don't stop. Just don't stop." Her simple encouragement has morphed into my running mantra when things get tough. This is how Jennifer helped me get started:

- I wrote down goals, dates and roughed-out plans. Writing it down made it real and not so danged scary.

- I told a handful of good friends. I reached out to the people who had watched me try and fail repeatedly, and loved me anyway. I called them and said, "I'm doing this, and I'm serious." Wade, Hannah, Liz, Deb, Anneke. I asked them to stick with me. I asked for permission to check in. I gave them permission to check in with me. I promised not to be defensive.

- I got approval from my doctor. When a patient expresses a firm desire and has a plan of action to try to get his/her health back, doctors are *super* supportive.

- I picked one thing at a time to work on. Small things like drinking more water, writing down what I ate, going for a walk each day. I picked one healthy habit and worked on it until I was comfortable that it wouldn't go away. Then I picked a new one to learn.

One of the early and important lessons I learned was that when you're talking big lifestyle changes, do not try to make a ton of changes all at the same time. I tried that. Gung ho, ready to fight and change my life. All the changes, right now. Making all the sweeping changes at once was a total, overwhelming disaster. It was simply too much change, too daunting. I had an epic, albeit short-lived, meltdown. My friend Wade took my frantic call and in his unfailingly calm manner, he strongly suggested that we should maybe focus on just *one* thing at a time. "Let's just take one concrete, healthy thing at a time, *one*," he said. "And freaking breathe, Bets. Just breathe."

One bite at a time. Just one small bite at a time. That is how I began to eat the elephant.

A Simple Plan

By June 2011, I was making a quantum mental shift. One that's still, to this day, terribly difficult to articulate. I finally understood that my diabetes was an entirely self-created, lifestyle disease. When the light bulb finally clicked on, I was horrified and shocked. I really, truly understood that I had done this to myself. I was tackled and flattened by my emotions: Shame. Fear. Anger. Embarrassment. Often all at the same time.

Being a grossly overweight diabetic was all on me. I had created this horrible predicament by myself. Damn. Yet for some inexplicable reason, slowly, hope began to surface. Rather than simply condemning myself, I began to see an opportunity. If I had done this to myself (and I absolutely had!), maybe there was a chance that I could undo or reverse this disease. Maybe. Was I willing and brave and stubborn enough to put in the work to try to beat it? Or at least to stop it from getting worse?

This might be a good time to talk about surgical options. I considered them. I went through the informational meeting and some of the initial counseling. For resolution of type 2 diabetes, the best surgical option within the bariatric surgical world at the time was what they called Roux-en-Y. I was sitting in a room with about 35 other morbidly obese people hearing about the mechanics of the surgery, the after care and critical importance of creating a new lifestyle, or the surgery would not be as successful as possible. The doctor spent some time outlining that new lifestyle. All stuff I hated and didn't want to do. I mean, I didn't want to be obese, but I wasn't ready to change my entire life around and give up my favorite foods.

I just wanted the surgery to cure me (Spoiler: "…bariatric surgery is a 'tool.' Weight Loss success also depends on many other important factors, such as nutrition, exercise, behavior modification, and more.' American Society for Metabolic and Bariatric Surgery.)

The doctor explained how we could no longer drink soda (about 30 of us in the room had some form of soda — likely not diet — with us), and had to stick to small, timed meals, and avoid certain foods. He also talked about the failure rate, including how many people die or develop nutritional deficiencies. But the statistic that caught my ear was the regaining-weight-after-surgery number. He said, depending on the source and how it was measured, 35 to 65 percent of patients gained most or all of the weight back. There seems to be a whole lot of supposition about why that is. In reading the literature and talking to some people who work in the bariatric surgical field, they all chime in with "those who succeed change their lifestyle, those who regain the weight usually are still doing all the same stuff they were doing pre-surgery."

The click in my brain felt audible to the outside world. *If I can do the wholesale lifestyle changes that have to be done once I have the surgery, then why the hell can't I make those changes NOW?!* I was done considering surgical options. They would work for others—and I respect that everyone has to make their own decisions about their body and their journey. I was going to embark on the only thing the doctors seemed to all agree would work for the long term: changing my lifestyle.

On July 2, 2011, I woke up determined to push my life in a very different direction, no matter what it took. I woke up resolute about my plan and with a changed heart. The switch had been flipped. I had a simple plan:

EAT LESS. MOVE MORE.

Or, to put it less politely:

EAT LESS CRAP. GET YOUR BUTT MOVING.

That was it. A new lifestyle. That was my exclusive focus. I didn't think about quality of food, or intensity of exercise, or special pills or surgeries or "magic bullets" or statistics. I merely put less food into my body, and tried to move more and more each and every day. It was simple—by no means easy—but simple.

So I started. I kept after it every day, stubborn as all get-out. Many of the early days on this journey sucked. I shed tears. I got angry. I got totally pissed off, as my old life and habits were shoved aside and unceremoniously ditched. I began eating less and making smarter food choices - looking for satiating, nutrient dense foods. I ditched fast food. I measured portions and counted calories. I wrote down everything I ate. I banned sweets. I chose leaner cuts of meat. I quit eating in my car. I became intentional and mindful about my eating experiences.

Then, as the weight started to come off, I began walking. Walking, walking, and more walking. Basic stuff.

Was my trigger point really tied to my mom's death? Was it the little things piling up? Was it just that I had finally found a spark of bravery and determination that I had never noticed before? I really don't know. I accept that it was more like a perfect storm, and I was finally ready. Perhaps that is too simple an answer to satisfy folks who are looking to be motivated for their own life changes. I believe it was the right things at the right time, and I had just enough guts to make a run for it.

Eat Less, Move More

By July 2011, I was down close to 300 pounds because of making grudgingly minor changes in my life so that I could manage diabetes for the past decade. I was considered well-controlled in the world of type 2 diabetes. Stable weight (even while still being obese), avoiding sugar in my diet, stable blood tests, and we weren't having to increase any of my meds.

July 2, 2011 started a new chapter in my quest for major life change. The next three-plus years would be a frantic, chaotic, and successful mess. When I woke up that morning, I was finally ready to do the work needed to make real changes. I wanted to get rid of this disease, not just live with it. It was a much different feeling than the forced enthusiasm and hope that were present when I usually started a new diet. This was different. *Entirely different*. This was soul-deep and relentless and essential. This time, I was not driven by fear or despair or guilt. My desire to live was finally bigger than my fears. My only goal was to reverse diabetes. To the casual observer my journey must have looked like a total shit show. But by God, it was *my* shit show.

Focused on that thought alone, I picked ideas that provoked and energized me:

- Reverse diabetes. Get rid of it.

- In choosing between losing weight or managing my blood sugar, I would choose the latter. Every time,

- I was not doing this to please anyone else. This was about saving my own life.

- There would be no excuses. None. I was going to own my journey.

- There would be no whining.

- I would give 100-percent effort.

- I would stay open-minded about solutions.

- I was not looking for quick fixes. This was about new habits and a permanent lifestyle shift.

I learned everything I could about food, exercise, and myself. I eventually zeroed in on a handful of ideas that continue to work:

- Continue to make exercise a habit and a priority in my life.

- Stay focused on the healthiest, smartest food choices for my needs and goals.

- Embrace the small handful of people in my life to whom I remain accountable. They have unconditional permission to remind me to get back on track.

- Consider food as fuel, not a reward.

- Say no to social situations where food will be an issue for me. I have come too far to take orders from a cookie.

Lifestyle Changes

I talked to my doctor and told her my plan: I was going to get off insulin and reverse diabetes by eating less and moving more. She sent me away for three months to lose weight and learn how to move more. She had to be genuinely skeptical that I would stick with it. I'd never stuck to it before. But I worked hard and showed her proof of my commitment. I went back weighing less and with improved numbers. I told her I had signed up for a 10K walk. I wasn't screwing around. I wanted off insulin. She could help me, or I would figure it out myself. I told her that, in those exact words. Then I asked her what our plan would be.

"Here's our plan," she said ...

Getting off all meds would take nearly two years. In May 2011, each day I was taking 72 units of Lantus via injection, two other injections, and five other oral medications to regulate sugars and other related issues that commonly plague diabetics.

We decreased insulin in small increments weekly, over many months. I reduced the daily bolus (the dosage), then we would watch my daily fasting numbers for about ten days. If my numbers stayed steady, I could decrease the bolus again — and repeat the process. There were periods of 25 days or longer when I could not lessen the dosage. I wasn't losing weight, my diet wasn't tight enough, I had been sick, or maybe I wasn't exercising consistently. I would figure out the issue, work to get it corrected, and we would start the process of dropping dosages again. At one point, it dawned on me that I was trading one kind of drug for another: food and exercise! Staying off diabetes meds would be totally dependent upon my maintaining these serious lifestyle changes. A bit overwhelming to consider.

As I continued to eat better and work my way off insulin, I started moving more. I was a hot, sweaty mess. All the time. And I didn't care what I looked like working out, or what anyone thought of me. I was beginning to see the scale and my glucose readings drop. I was seeing results that strengthened my resolve and dedication. I learned to run. I bought a bike. I started lifting weights. I met Josh and Wendie Gum and started learning to run trails with them. Then I met Spencer, who became my running coach. I was buying real running shoes, then actually running in them.

And then the day that I had been working for arrived. I took my last shot of insulin on February 4, 2012. By May 2013, I was off all meds. And in October 2014, my doc spoke the most incredible words: "You are no longer diabetic." She gave me a hug. She told me I could put my glucose testing kit in a drawer. I weighed 175 and my BMI (body mass index) was "normal." My A1c was the lowest it had ever been. Both of us were proudest of that single number, which was all because of diet and exercise. It reflected my changed lifestyle. I had chased a low A1c for more than a decade, and I had finally caught it.

It has been a journey and an adventure, and the hardest work of my life. I know that it will continue to be a fight, for all the remaining days of my life. I am not out of the woods. I am not done. There are still hurdles. That's okay. I'm up for the fight.

My doctor said that in her 20-plus years of practicing medicine, she had only a small handful of patients work their way off substantial meds without surgical intervention. Several times, she has had to research our next step, as this wasn't a common situation. It's kind of cool to be the challenging patient in a good way.

Will I be able to stay off insulin for the rest of my life? That's unlikely. Research indicates that diabetes will re-emerge at some point. So I consider it in remission. If old habits return, so will the disease. Meanwhile, the longer I can go without insulin, the longer I can keep tight control on blood sugars, the longer I can go without causing collateral harm to my eyes, heart, and kidneys — the better for me!

I left my doctor's office that day and walked to my car, where I bawled out of happiness for about ten minutes. The odds had been against me, big time. I had purposely ignored that fact for several years. It was finally hitting me. The best feeling of all was knowing I had developed solid habits I could use to keep healthy and active for the rest of my life. I got home, hugged and chatted with my dad, and ate a healthy dinner. The next morning, I got up early to go for a celebration run with Hannah and Spencer.

Life with Scabs

Little things happened along the way that let me know my body really was healing and functioning normally. And would affirm how sick I really had been with diabetes.

Like scabs.

I was running down a hill on a Thursday-night group run in the spring of 2016, looking at the stunning forest. The fields were alive with flowers and I was laughing with friends. It was the first time we'd seen the sun in something like 2,000 days. Okay, maybe 200. But I was feeling soooo goooood, outside in the sun, running!

Then I fell. One moment I was running, the next I was on my face, kissing the dirt. There was no sensation of falling, no chance to catch myself. It is a hazard of our sport, and it wasn't my first fall. My friends, Mark and Sarah, heard me crash and helped pick me up. We quickly figured out I'd tripped on seemingly thin air. Sarah, being a good friend, charitably pointed to a twig about the size of a dried-up earthworm and suggested that had done it.

Somehow, yet again, I had totally avoided all the major land mines that I could have fallen upon. Roots or rocks could easily have smashed my head, or broken a wrist or rib. I could have had far greater body damage. Nope. I landed on one tiny rock and a bunch of dirt. I was very lucky. I broke a finger and tore up a knee. It knocked the breath out of me. Minor damage.

And it started a fascinating social experiment of contrasting my "before" life with my "new" life. It all had to do with healing and scabs.

One of the things that had alerted doctors to my diabetes was a lack of healing with sores. I thought back to the start of my diagnosis, when I got a blister on my foot. Six months later, the wound specialist was speculating about whether to cut off part of my foot. Increasing doses of varied antibiotics weren't working. It stayed infected and never scabbed up. It refused to heal.

Indeed, when my sugars were high, healing from anything was slow — if not nearly impossible. This is because high or uncontrolled glucose levels impair healing. According to the American Diabetes Association website, "Higher or poorly controlled glucose control means a wound cannot receive adequate nutrients or oxygen, resulting in slower and less effective wound healing. Nerves in the body of a diabetic patient are affected when blood-glucose levels are uncontrolled, which leads to a loss of sensation or diabetic neuropathy."

The first year I was learning to run, I was still trying to get off insulin and figure out how to use food and exercise instead of drugs. I was still diabetic. I would carefully, compulsively check my feet after every run. With diabetic neuropathy in both feet, I cannot to this day feel significant portions of either foot. I have ripped off an entire toenail and never knew it until I took my shoe off (trail running friends are like, "Cool! That's so lucky not to have feeling in your damn toes!"). While I was managing diabetes, my feet could get hurt and I wouldn't feel it. Weeks could go by with me having an open wound.

Fast forward to my downhill faceplant on the trail that happened on a Thursday, three days later and — wait for it — I had scabs! I was healing fast and well. It stunned me. My healthy body is kind of badass sometimes. It continues to amaze me. The likelihood of me having ruined major organs, and really doing major damage to my body as a diabetic, was huge. And yet, there I was, with a self-inflicted trail wound healing beautifully and fast. I was healing like a normal person. Who knew a scab could be exciting? It was such a sign of progress and healing for me, and I was thrilled.

X Marks the Spot

I got a tattoo in San Francisco one weekend. I mean, why not? I had just finished a big, bucket-list racing event: my first 50K trail race at the North Face Endurance Challenge in the hills just north of the Golden Gate Bridge. My friends Wendie Gum and Jeff Sherman were getting tattoos too. We were done with the race and being tourists for a day or two.

Well, there is a little more to the story: a little heart tattoo on the outside of my left foot marks the spot where my diabetes diagnosis began. Back in the early 2000s, I was wearing cute shoes to a work conference. While totally adorable, those shoes gave me a nasty blister. Three months later, the blister still had not healed. In fact, it was infected, and the wound site was growing. I was referred to a wound-care specialist. At the same time, I was being told that I had full-blown type 2 diabetes. The wound-care folks were talking about treatment options being limited because of my illness. The words "partial amputation" will always haunt me.

At one point in that first year of my diabetes diagnosis, my sister was going to get a tattoo. I had always wanted one. I was slowly beginning to get my blood sugars under control. I mentioned off-handedly to my doc at the time (not the one who ultimately helped me reverse the disease) that I was going to get a tattoo with my sister. I remember his response: "That is the single, stupidest thing I have ever heard. You have a team of people who barely saved your foot because you cannot heal, and you want to purposely inflict a new open wound on your body? Find a new doctor!"

40

Um, okay ... so maybe I didn't need a tattoo (I needed, and eventually found, a new doctor!). I buried the idea of a tattoo for more than a decade.

When I saw my current doctor, and she told me I was no longer diabetic, I asked her if it would be okay for me to get a tattoo. I told her I wanted a reminder of my diabetes journey and the fact that I was never, ever slipping back to my old ways. She tilted her head to the side and said, "I would get that tattoo on my foot, if I were you!" So that's what I did. And it reminds me each time I see it how grateful I am to still have that part of my foot.

2 CHAPTER TWO
TOO FAT TO EXERCISE

I was convinced I was too fat to exercise.

When I talk with people facing mega weight loss, this topic always emerges as a core frustration, embarrassment, or concern. It was one of my central concerns for over a decade. The mental hurdles are just as fearsome as the physical. How do you get your mind to quiet down so you can get your butt to the gym and get started? It seems to be a radically different tipping point for everyone.

My tipping point came when I finally understood that food alone was not going to get me where I was trying to go. If I was to control diabetes, exercise had to be added. Muscles have an important role in helping the body process insulin. I had to get moving. It took six months from the moment I learned I had to add exercise to when I actually set foot in the gym. That's half of a year of battling the demons in my head. When you are obese and totally out of shape, and you finally take the big, brave step to join the world of the physically active, you feel vulnerable beyond belief. Indeed, I felt ragged and mentally exhausted even before I set foot in the gym.

For over ten years, these were among the "I am too fat to be seen trying to exercise" thoughts that were zinging around in my mind:

- Fat people don't belong in the world of fit and thin people. I had plenty of personal experiences and endless marketing and advertising examples to tell me that "we" (the overweight) are not welcome and do not belong.

- I am desperately afraid someone is going to mock me, laugh at me, or otherwise be mean.

- It will be ugly. I am not a pretty crier. I am not a pretty "sweater."

- I am beyond help. I don't know where to start. Why bother, at this point?

- Thin people are disgusted by fat people. I do not want to see the look of pity or disgust when I wind up next to them on a treadmill at the gym.

- I will have to shower after working out. Which means I have to be naked. The likelihood of having the locker room all to myself is about *zero*. Which means: Kill me now.

Baby Steps

Think about how a child learns to walk. Children crawl. They pull themselves up on things so they can stand assisted. Then they attempt to let go—halting, uncertain, but with determined focus. Throw in a few temper tantrums, plenty of falling down and getting back up. Through countless failed attempts, they will not give up. Then one step leads to two and, before you know it, they're off and running with abandon.

When I started this journey, I was taking lots of baby steps. They genuinely felt like huge, monster steps to me. Turns out they were just the right bite-sized pieces I needed to get to the much bigger goal. I was down to 285 pounds from a high of about 399. I was still taking three shots a day and handfuls of pills. Walking to the office from my car took genuine effort. The only way I was ever going to build a healthy, active lifestyle was to break my changes down into tiny, manageable, must-not-panic-and-quit pieces.

These were some of the baby steps:

- I parked farther away from the office, from the grocery store, from the mall. I no longer searched for the nearest parking spots.

- I took the stairs even when it meant I would show up for a meeting with a sweaty head, red face, and gasping for air. I carried baby wipes and a bandana in my bag. No excuses.

- I wore a pedometer every day and tried to hit 5,000 steps. Then 10,000. Then 15,000.

- I put on workout clothes and went for walks on purpose at least three days a week. That was over and above the pedometer steps.

- I picked meeting spots that were as far away from my office as possible, so I was required to walk. Given that I tend to cut timing close, it was always a brisk walk.

- I turned lunches and coffee meetings into conversational walks with willing and understanding coworkers.

Baby steps. Adding just a little at a time.

I'm often asked how long my first run was. What was my "starting mileage?" I explain that for years, I merely walked. A lot. Then I walked faster and I walked farther. I worked on walking before I ever tried to run a step. And when I ran? I wanted to be able to run between telephone poles. I made it across a driveway. My starting mileage was in feet. Feet! I was proud of that. I still am, to be honest! I abso-freaking-lutely walked a ton before I ever, ever tried to run. Baby steps is what this whole adventure was really about.

Worm Walks

In the process of finding a healthy life, I discovered that I love to run.

When I say this to people who insist they hate to exercise, I may be greeted with stares of incredulity. "I hate to exercise." Sometimes it's said off-handedly, sometimes with intense emotion. Usually it's said with a tone of apology or a plea for sympathy. I used to hate exercise, too. My mantra was, "Run when chased." Even then, if I stood any kind of chance, I would much rather stop and fight back. I had no desire to run, or take gym classes, or lift weights. I had no fitness. I hated to sweat.

Times have changed. Times can change. It obviously took some serious baby steps to change things. I was 399 pounds and inactive. Now I'm at a healthy weight and I love to run. How did that happen? How did I learn to love running? How did I learn to make exercise a priority and a habit?

The honest answer is boring: I learned to love running by walking.

I started walking with my friend Hannah O'Leary, years before I began my lifestyle overhaul. Hannah is a runner, a serious runner. She has run the

Boston Marathon. She has solidly healthy habits and is someone who, for years, I looked up to. She was by my side early on this journey. She's an artist, a world-class photographer and one of the toughest, most stubborn women I know. Our early walks were labors of love and times to chat. We would meet at the Oregon State University campus in the morning, several days a week, and just walk. Slowly. Short distances. She would encourage and push me to walk just a little farther each time we met. Over the years, these became the famous "worm walks."

It rains a lot in western Oregon. Worms lay all over the sidewalks and footpaths. When you are grossly overweight and out of shape, the act of pretending to save each and every worm you encounter is a brief, welcomed rest period. Trust me, it was a horrible, obvious stalling tactic. She knew what I was doing and pretended otherwise. We now joke about those early "worm walks." Getting in a mile was a 30 minute endeavor. Thousands of worms were spared.

With Hannah's help, being active became a consistent endeavor. A daily walk with my friend slowly became a habit that I truly enjoyed and looked forward to. After a few months of walking, I began to measure and observe things:

- How much farther could we go?

- How fast were we going?

- How many miles had we covered in a week?

- Why were my blood sugars better on the days we walked?

- Wow! I can walk and talk at the same time, without gasping for air!

I had no idea that the worm walks were the beginning of a lifestyle change.

On January 1, 2012, with my lifestyle overhaul in full swing, Hannah and I signed up for a race—one where I could walk. It had generous time limits. Hannah knew that having a race to look forward to was important, as it would keep me focused on staying active. I had not yet figured that out. But I knew that training for an event kept things fun. That's important when you're doing hard, repetitive work. Plus, we got free T-shirts! Win-win! I walked that first race, a 10K. I was the last person to finish. I was sore for days. But I felt invincible. I had done it!

*My first 10K. Hannah walked it with me. I was about 280
pounds and still injecting insulin*

So I took the logical next step. I signed up for a marathon. *What*? A *marathon*?

The Maui Oceanfront Marathon was only the second event that I had ever signed up for. I planned to walk the whole thing. I remember when I told Hannah. The conversation went something like this:

"Ummm ... You signed up for a marathon that happens in 11 months?!"

"Yes!"

"Bets, you have not yet even done a half marathon!"

"I know. I am going to walk it. You'll train with me. I can do this!"

"Yes. Yes, you can! We really have to get training!"

That is a living example of unwavering support and friendship. If Hannah had any thoughts besides pure support and encouragement, I never knew it. She helped me understand training plans, made sure I had good shoes and lectured me about not wearing cotton (because of chafing). I couldn't have done it without her. The marathon, including the months of training, was an incredible experience.

Post Maui Oceanfront Marathon. My hair is short in the picture; it was growing back after insulin-induced hair loss the previous spring.

Some of the best changes in our lives can happen simply because we choose to face our fears. Signing up for a marathon was facing my fears. Having a friend to walk by my side made it possible. And it changed everything. Hannah was as eager to celebrate my goals and successes as she was her own. We slogged out the long, slow training miles in cheerful companionship. She understood the daily balance I was trying to find between fear and reason and learning to make being active a lifelong habit. And even though I suspect she knew all along that I was just stopping to catch my breath, she always let me stop and pick up worms to "save" them.

Thousands of worms.

You have to walk before you can run.

A woman approached me at work and asked how to get started running. I answered with generic, supportive words like, "Take the training slow," "Get good shoes," "Look online for a training plan," and "You can do this!" She listened and then said, "Yes ... Betsy, I get that it will take a while to learn to run any distance. That I can't give up. But how did you actually *start* physically running?"

I had to really think back to what it was like when I took those first awkward, shuffling steps. It started with driveways and telephone poles. I'd been walking with focus and intent for several months. I was working on walking longer distances at faster speeds. I'd walked several 10Ks by this point. I lived in farm country. From our farm to the stop sign was 2.43 miles (3.9 kilometers), round trip. Five houses on the road, no shoulder on the road, one annoying dog, some railroad tracks. The roads were usually empty.

When I finally decided I wanted to learn how to run, I picked a short distance and gave it a shot. I planned to jog between two telephone poles on our road. I made it across the width of our neighbor's driveway. That was it. Those telephone poles suddenly seemed miles apart. I jogged the driveway and then I walked to the stop sign. When I got back to our neighbor's driveway, I forced myself to jog back across. In the next few days and weeks, I forced myself to add a few running steps each day. By the next month, I was still struggling, but I was jogging between those damned telephone poles. And I had a huge grin on my face. I was not discouraged.

When I tell this story, there may be no response I hear more often than "You must have been so discouraged to have such slow progress!" And at first, that statement really offended me. To be sure, I had moments of wondering what in hell I was doing. But what I wanted, what I was working very hard to create, was a whole new lifestyle. And I was being chased by diabetes. I was in a very real race for my life. I was motivated.

The fact that it took me a month to hit my initial goal of jogging between telephone poles? I saw it as a victory. I had not given up. I was not discouraged with the time it took to reach that goal. I just wanted to jog between those two stupid poles and be able to say I did it. Eventually, I nailed my goal. But then I didn't stop with the telephone poles. I kept looking for new landmarks. I remember the first time I ran all the way to the stop sign, 1.21 miles. And then the time I ran to the stop sign and back again. I kept picking landmarks. I made a game out of pushing myself to get there as fast as I could. Those first physical steps were really, truly that small. But that is how I started running. And for the record? I still play the landmark game when I'm pushing to something new, or I am tired or struggling just to get to that bend in the road, that tree, that rock in the road. Just one more step. It works every time.

... And Loving It!

Running is not for everyone. And that's okay. The real issue is not running, anyway. Let's be honest. The key to healthy, sustainable success is to fall in love with some form of physical activity that you will consistently make time for. It should be something active, fun, and rewarding. It can be friend-based or solitude-giving. You may love swimming or hiking or cycling or walking or Zumba.

It does not have to be running. It just has to be something. That is the secret. Being active is what I fell in love with. It's what really changed my life. That activity just happens to be running. Before I learned to love running, this was my mindset: run when chased. And even then, run only if you don't stand a fighting chance. But when I was challenged to explain what it was about running that led me to say I hated it, the truth that grudgingly emerged was that I'd never actually tried it.

Soon I was having some honest conversations with myself about how I could hate something I knew nothing about, and with which I had no experience. This was my reasoning: I had been overweight my entire life. Overweight people don't run. Overweight people who try to run look pathetically ridiculous and are made fun of, brutally so. And I was not just overweight. I was morbidly obese. Therefore, I hated running. With a passion. If I told people I hated running, they would assume I'd tried it, and I was just choosing not to run. They would never, ever guess that I said I hate running because I'm fat and scared, and I knew it was beyond any fitness level I ever had in my life. It was beyond any amount of work or fitness that I could possibly begin to imagine.

So I had a few weeks of struggling with the topic. Then I finally had to admit to myself I was deeply afraid of something I'd never bothered to try. It's a rough process to acknowledge something about yourself that reveals you to be weak. This time, I was not going to run (figuratively or literally) from my fears. It was time to put on my big-girl panties and deal with things (disclaimer: like a lot of my female running friends, I don't wear underwear with my running tights. "Big-girl panties" is just a figure of speech for this commando-runner.).

Running, for me, sucked at the start. Let's get that out of the way. By this time, I weighed about 255 pounds. Running was physically painful and mentally exhausting. I promised myself that this time, I'd give running a really solid effort and at least get past the fear to allow myself a personally informed opinion. I pulled a beginners' running plan off the internet, wore the best compression gear to contain my belly fat rolls, made time for running each day, set mini-goals, told some friends. I honestly, wholeheartedly tried running. I kept working to build distance and time. I would sweat so heavily I was drenched, no matter the time of year. My face would turn an alarming beet red, and people would ask if I was alright. I would be red-faced and sweating for hours after working out. My feet, legs, and hips would ache for days. I had to put up with mean catcalls from car windows. My appetite went through the roof and I really had to watch my food consumption to keep the scale creeping downward. I had to invest in better shoes, bras, and specialty compression gear. But after a few weeks of giving it my all ... I kind of fell for it!

I loved the challenge. I loved feeling the accomplishment. I loved the people I was meeting, all of them unabashedly supportive. I loved how my blood sugars would swoop low and stay there. I loved how I felt a fierce sense of pride in my body, and what I was asking her (yes, I refer to my body as a her) to do. I loved that my body was working harder than ever. I wondered just how much more I could do.

I kept pushing. And learning. And meeting great people. And running farther and farther. My love for running was not a love-at-first-sight kind of thing. It was a two-year-plus process of stubbornly not giving up. As far as I'm concerned, the key to learning to love running was deciding I wanted something more than I was afraid of it.

There are legitimate physical issues that prevent people from running. Trust me, I get it. I'm not here to ask you to do something you physically shouldn't be doing. But I will ask a much bigger question, the one I had to ask myself: what are you afraid of? For me, running was something I feared. That's why I thought I hated it. But turns out I didn't hate running—I hated being made fun of. I was afraid I would look dumb. I was paralyzed by where and how to even start. I was terrified people would pity me, or mock me, or be disgusted by me.

I was afraid of something I'd never tried. Once I tried it—really, truly gave it an honest effort—it began to change my life, and it's helped to save it. That first step is always the hardest. It was so worth braving it.

Bra Runs Amok

Women who are active and endowed with certain "charms" need bionic-level sports bras. No way around it. I have become somewhat of an expert on sports bras since deciding I wanted to live an active life. Let's call it necessity. Or self-defense. Let me tell you a story ...

My friend Anneke told me several times early in my lifestyle-change journey that I needed to get a good sports bra. Her exact words to me were "Betsy. *Do not* run to Walmart and buy a cheap, uni-boob, stretchy sports bra. They don't provide support. Spend the money and buy a decent bra."

I was losing weight and getting smaller and smaller. I was *not* going to spend 50-plus dollars on a bra I could wear for two months, if that. So I ran to Walmart and bought a cheap, uni-boob, stretchy sports bra. I didn't tell Anneke.

Prior to learning they made sports bras in plus sizes, or that I really did need a special bra for running/jumping/moving, I was simply doubling up my regular bras, a common practice for larger-busted and/or overweight women. I have a feeling I'm the only one dumb enough to publicly admit to this practice. You do what you have to do. Anyway, I signed up for a boot-camp class led by my friend, Amy. Her fitness boot-camp classes were well known in our area for being super fun and a welcoming spot for all abilities. About 75-100 people in a gym all jumping and moving and sweating. Fantastic music.

Everyone having a great time for an intense hour of cardio.

I and my new sports bra went to her class. About fifteen minutes in, we did something called a "burpee." Variations abound, but the basic concept is this: You start by standing up straight, quickly drop to a push-up position, do the push-up, hop back up quickly and then with your hands over your head, you jump for the sky. Repeat multiple times. *Fast, fluid, strong.*

I did the push-up part of the burpee and when we got to the "jump for the sky" part…

All hell broke loose.

When I landed, my "girls" unceremoniously tumbled out of the *bottom* of the handy-dandy sports bra The cheap piece-of-crap bra then proceeded to quickly and tightly roll itself up toward my neck. *Kind of like an old-fashioned window shade.* So, standing in the back of Amy's class with everyone doing burpees, I was being choked by my bra.

And my boobs were very decidedly *not* in the bra.

I was a sweaty mess. In a form-fitting workout shirt. Boobs loose. Bra choking me. I tried to discreetly unravel the bra from my neck and armpits. It became obvious that it was *not* going to happen. At this point, I was on the verge of hysterical laughter. Not tears. I knew full well this was both comical and totally stupid. I also had no real clue how to undo this holy-freaking-sweaty mess without having to walk through what felt like 1,000 people to the bathroom on the other side of the gym—which suddenly felt bigger than a football field. I had no choice. I crossed my arms and made a red-faced hobble-dash for the safety of the bathroom. I got everything in place where it belonged. I quickly went back out to the class and gave it half-hearted gusto, keeping my arms glued strategically to my sides. I got home and promptly tossed the bra in the trash can with some creative language thrown in for kicks. I silently vowed never to tell a word of this story to Anneke. Ever. Until now.

I immediately set out on a mission to find a better sports bra so I could keep going to boot camp with Amy. Over the next year or so I tried just about every bra they made in my size with varying degrees of success. Mercifully, there were no more epic, public failures. About a year later, I was wholeheartedly trying to learn to run. And it was, uh, apparent that I would need a really good sports bra. Better than the ones I had found on my own at that point. I needed one that had exceptional motion control, would protect my back, and would not chafe me. I asked Spencer, my new running coach, to *please* connect me with any of the local female athletes he knew so I could ask them a question. He introduced me to Taryn Hand. Taryn is an athlete and dietician. She also happened to be working at a running store at the time. I sent a quick email with far too many personal details, and within a day or two she had me in a great running bra. One I could run, jump, and move around in with no issues! It fit perfectly! To this day, that bra has never betrayed me. And trust me, I've put it to the test.

So, the *moral of this story*? Burpees are bad for you (*kidding!*). *Listen to your friends who are speaking from hard-earned experience. Invest in a good sports bra.*

3 CHAPTER THREE
COACHING

When I met Spencer, I had already lost more than 150 pounds and was off insulin. Clearly, I was well into my lifestyle revamp. I was super-focused, working to get off all other oral meds, and intent on losing another 50 pounds. And I was falling in love with being able to move! Running, in particular, had begun to capture my heart. We were introduced randomly at work. "Hey," said a colleague, "you both run. You know each other, right?" We didn't, even with 100 mutual friends. Here I was, a 230-pound woman who was starting to get serious about running. I was introduced to a tall, thin, very fit dude who looked every bit a hard-core runner.

Spencer asked me earnestly, "You run?!"

"Um, er, ah … I'm really not *that* kind of runner." I continued with confidence and intelligence (not so much). I think I said in a single, rushed breath, "I can't run like you obviously can run. I'm really, really slow. I just want to be able to run a mile without walking." Spencer responded, "It's cool that you run! Let's grab coffee and talk about running."

So we did. I told him my story, how I'd lost a great deal of weight, how I'd weaned myself from insulin, how I'd decided I wanted to be a runner. It was not about sticking to a specific diet, this was about lifestyle changes. I confessed that I couldn't run more than a mile or two. But I told him my deepest heart's desire: I wanted to someday run an ultra. Had he heard of ultras? Did he know I was talking about any running event over a 50K distance? I was waiting for him to laugh at me, or give me the pity look that said "people your size don't run."

With a genuine ear-to-ear grin, Spencer responded, "Yeah, I've heard of them." He hadn't laughed at me, so I went ahead and asked what I thought was the elephant-in-the room question: did he really think it possible that someone like me might someday run an ultra? Could I someday run 100 miles? "Absolutely!" he said with no hesitation.

Wow. Someone believes in me as I am right now. That was a brand-freaking-new feeling.

Had he heard of ultras? Geez. It turns out he'd run them! The world of ultrarunning isn't very big. No firm stats, but the best we can figure is about .02 percent of the population actually runs them. With dumb luck, I had somehow stumbled into one of those rarities. And he was only the second person who had greeted my ultra goal with a positive response, not the standard ones: "You're crazy!" "Your ovaries will fall out!" "Running ruins your knees." He asked me what I was doing to train. I told him I was running and hiking and biking and weightlifting and going to boot-camp classes. If a little is good, a lot is better, right?

"You're doing a lot," Spencer said. "You might want to be careful and maybe look at some structure. It will keep you from getting hurt." My brain shut down at his words of caution. I was so, so tired of everyone preaching at me to be careful. Diabetes was trying to kill me; caution seemed stupid. Couldn't people see that I was going to win this war against diabetes, if everyone would just get the hell out of my way?!

As it turned out, I was just about to reach a very real breaking point. In June of that year, 2013, I literally hit the ground. I passed out in Safeway. An off-duty fireman walking in the same grocery aisle broke my fall when he saw me weaving for a few steps. I wound up in the emergency room. The diagnosis was exhaustion and potassium depletion. "Hang up your running shoes for a few weeks," the doctors told me, "and give your body a break."

A few days later, I met Spencer again for coffee. I was wearing a portable EKG/heart monitor. I felt defeated and scared to death that I was going to lose my foothold on this new lifestyle. I needed help. And I was more than ready to listen. I really wanted to be a runner. Blacking out scared the crap out of me. I clearly didn't know what the hell I was doing, after all. I asked Spencer about structure and preventing this from happening again. I asked him about coaching. Spencer was not coaching anyone at that point. He was adamant about it. He offered to help me find a coach. But after some follow-up conversations, I flat-out begged him to consider working with me. Finally, he agreed we could give it a try ... for a short period of time. I ditched the EKG/heart monitor after a ton of tests. I got a totally clean bill of health after a period of serious rest. I had permission to resume exercising and running, slowly and cautiously. Together with Spencer's help, I was committed to learning the basics and rebuilding my fitness habits in a healthy, sustainable, safe way.

If you were to ask Spencer how our coaching partnership worked, he would tell you there was lots of cursing, learning curves, and sassy moments. It was a struggle to trust another person to help me on this journey. He had to practice a whole lot of patience with me. Even harder than learning how to run was accepting and learning that Spencer was on my side and no question was a dumb one. I had to be honest with him about what I was thinking and feeling. This whole journey of changing one's entire lifestyle can be lonely and relentless. You get used to doing a lot of it on your own, without crowd approval, without understanding or support from anyone beyond a small handful of trusted friends. You get used to battling prevalent shame. To invite Spencer into this journey, and then relinquish some portion of control, was a very big step for me.

Coaching worked for me. Under Spencer's coaching I've learned the basics, pushed boundaries, cemented some good habits, run a whole bunch of events, including that 100-miler I dreamed about from the beginning. I'm currently training for other epic adventures. Coaching was just what I wanted and needed. And six years later, Spencer remains the perfect coach for me. His coaching extended well beyond running. He taught me how to *be coached*.

Me, Rita, Spencer. A training weekend in the Siskiyou Mountains.

Swimming ("I want to do an Ironman someday...")

It started with a conversation I had with my dad. I was telling him that my friends Joe Van V and Josh Gum did Ironman events. I admire the hell out of those two. I admitted that I was kinda-sorta wanting to compete in an Ironman too. In the unlikely event you don't know what an Ironman is, it's the ultimate triathlon: a 2.4-mile swim, a 112-mile bicycle ride, and a marathon 26.2-mile run, raced in order and without a break.

I wanted to do an Ironman someday, yet I couldn't swim. I had never been able to do more than float and dog paddle. Three days after our conversation, my dad called me out. "Bets," he said. "I've been thinking about something you said the other day. And it's total bullshit. You can learn to swim just like you learned to run and bike and control diabetes and lose weight. So quit saying you can't, and figure out a way to learn how."

Alrighty, then. I got called out by my dad.

From a friend, I got the name of a well-respected swim coach (well-respected for working with terrified beginners who happen to be adults.). I didn't call for three months, and when I did, I didn't follow up. Then I purposefully forgot all about it. But things you've left in the dust sometimes have a way of catching up with you. A year or two later, a man walked up to me at an event and introduced himself. "I'm Troy," he said. "You may not remember, but a long time ago, you called me about being your swim coach. Are you ready to start lessons?"

Gulp. The truth is, I'm afraid of water. I'm scared of trying to breathe and having water nearby—like, anywhere near my face. I confessed. I told Troy about this near-phobia I have with water, as a lame way of explaining why I'd never followed through after my initial contact. He assured me he would be able to help me learn to swim. The part I didn't tell him was about my body-image issues. I was fearful of being seen in a swimsuit by, oh, any other human being. I would be dragging a ton of baggage with me into the pool.

Nevertheless, Troy and I set up a time to get swim lessons started. And for days before, I was ridiculously nervous. When I don't learn things instantly or see profound progress, I get frustrated with myself. As some of my good friends will say, I'm not easy to get along with when I'm scared or embarrassed. Troy is approaching sainthood to have hung in with me through the entire process.

For weeks, I was literally having panic attacks and hyperventilating during freestyle swims — even though I could literally touch the bottom of the pool at any given moment, anywhere in the lap pool. More than a few times, I dramatically flopped on the deck of the pool in tears. I have to admit, it got much better. While I still battled some fear about breathing near the water, I gained confidence. As I told Troy after the fourth or fifth lesson, "I think the lifeguards are finally looking a little more relaxed when I'm in the pool." Lesson ten was a really good one for me, mentally. As I arrived at the end of a lap, still struggling with breathing and gasping for air, Troy said, "You just have to get comfortable with the learning."

Yes! This was not just about swimming; it was about learning! I felt that a lightbulb had clicked on. Even though there were so many things for me to remember, including how to stay calm as I moved in the water, Troy reminded me that I needed to simply appreciate the process of learning something new. To get comfortable, once again, with the bumps and bruises and non-linear flow and fun of learning.

I can give myself a small measure of grace for simply facing my fears, and really trying to learn to swim. I can give myself some forgiveness for getting one thing right, even if I get five things wrong. I can give myself a dose of patience for learning a new skill while keeping up my other training. I can laugh at, and with, myself as I learn. Troy helped me to enjoy the process. I was too blind to the mechanics of a totally new sport, and of my vivid fear of water, and hating my body in a bathing suit to see what he had really been trying to teach me.

After some reflection, I knew that I really wanted to focus on embracing and loving the very process of learning. I loved learning how to run. I loved learning how to control blood sugars successfully. I loved learning how to ride a bike and how to do a sit-up. I struggled in the moment, and certainly hated parts of those processes; but I eventually embraced the deeper sense of accomplishment gleaned from really understanding and learning a new skill.

From the very start of our lessons, I told Troy that I had big goals: I wanted to do an Ironman. I wanted swimming in my "tool kit" for cross-training. I wanted to squash my fear of water. I wanted to be able to swim for cardio work, should I sustain a running or bicycling injury. And yet, I told him, what I wanted most from learning to swim was I wanted to be one of those funny, sassy, 90-year-old ladies rocking the swim cap, confident in her swimsuit, and kicking everyone's ass in a slow, methodical lap fest that lasts for hours.

Scaling Back

Most of what I see online about obesity is crap aimed at "helping" people feel as though there is a quick or effortless answer to weight loss, or aggressive marketing to sell the "magic bullet" to health and weight loss. So many lies and false-hope schemes. Meanwhile, largely absent is discussion about managing and solving the oncoming tidal wave of issues, even though statistics show that more than 68 percent of the U.S. population is overweight or obese.

There's a lot of information about quick fixes, "losing weight and getting healthy," or "loving who we are no matter what we look like." There is not a lot of discussion about solving the core issues — the hard truths — surrounding the topic of obesity. These are brutally difficult discussions to have because they are about people, their bodies, and their very personal relationships with food, health, and society.

Take me, for example. People approached me periodically about my weight. No matter what anyone tried to say, or how they tried to say it, all I ever heard was this:

"Betsy, I can see that you are fat. I don't know if you know that. Being fat is not a smart life choice. It's not healthy. I'm sure no one has ever told you that. Research backs me up."

"I see a heart attack waiting to happen. I see that you are physically uncomfortable with every breath you take. And while you keep yapping about how happy and content you are, I think you're protesting so loudly because you're trying to convince yourself that being fat and unhealthy is okay."

"I think you're too lazy to do the work to make your life different. Why can't you do a little work to try to save your own life? Why can't you just eat less and get moving?"

Endless variations on these types of conversations never went well, no matter who was delivering the message. It didn't matter how it was phrased, or how loving or well-intentioned it might have been. I really think my "advisers," such as they were, thought I would listen — that I wouldn't be defensive and would immediately change everything I was doing.

Yeah. Right.

When someone tried to talk to me about losing weight, I'd listen, thank them politely for their concern, be utterly humiliated, and go find comfort food — lots of comfort food. Then I would spend the rest of my life avoiding the person who tried to talk to me.

For years, I hid from the conversations, real or imaginary. I demanded that I be accepted exactly as I was, that society at large (pun intended) had a problem with "fat acceptance." Not me. It wasn't my problem if they couldn't accept what I looked like. For decades, I was part of the population of obese people with related health problems. I didn't want to face the core issues of my obesity and subsequent lifestyle-induced diabetes. I wanted to convince those around me that I was fine. I desperately wanted everyone to think I was a beautiful human, inside and out. And there were endless conversations with friends as I looked for affirmation that I was indeed loved and worthy, no matter my size. From where I sit now, I can see that all my posturing and fervent hoping was simply a way to avoid the core issues I faced.

Group Dynamics

Conversations with people who are chasing down new and healthy lifestyles almost always find their way to the topic of exercise — how to learn to love running or another activity. The top question I get is, "How do you make exercise a permanent part of your life?"

The answer is pretty simple.

1. Make time in your daily routine

2. Find accountability partners

3. Sign up for classes

4. Have a goal

When I gather with others who tackle the same challenges as I do, we rehash all the tricks that work. Individually, though, my fellow pilgrims on life-changing journeys often express the same underlying concern: they want to start running. They know they will be more successful in learning how, and sticking to the habit, if they join walks or runs with other people. But they're worried and embarrassed and fearful.

"People will make fun of me," they say. "They'll get frustrated at having to wait for me because I'm slow." "Maybe I should wait until I'm in shape and thin before trying to run with anyone." "I won't be able to keep up."

I remember those fears with stark clarity. I was in the same boat when I started. I'll admit that I even periodically dip my toes back into those waters of self-doubt, especially if I'm tired, intimidated, or trying something new. I become fearful and apologetic. The layers of fear and trepidation and hesitation were more suffocating than the layers of fat I was wearing. Here's the advice I pass along. Even now, I work to keep these thoughts front and center in my brain:

- Find a group or person that specifically says, "Everyone welcome." Take them at their word.

- Be honest about your abilities and goals. If you can run a 14-minute mile, and you are working to run two miles back-to-back, tell them! No shame, no bragging, no apologies. If you won't be able to keep up, or they know of another group that's more your speed, they will tell you!

- Plan to have fun! Enjoy being outside with other people who love to be active. The enthusiasm of being around people who love what they're doing is contagious. Try to leave your insecurities and discomfort and fears in your car. Be positive about what you think you'll experience. You will be surprised how often your expectations become reality.

- Finally, and perhaps most importantly, do not apologize. Groups that run with a variety of abilities often have preset, mid-run spots where you'll regroup. When you reach the lead group of runners, do not apologize for being the last to arrive or for making them wait. You're giving 100 percent of your best effort. You're moving and trying and growing and being brave, and they know it. They're happy you are there with them. I promise you this is the truth.

Apologizing highlights your insecurities. Chronic apologizers can be tiresome for even the hardiest, most supportive of souls. I know. I spent decades apologizing. For being fat. For being in someone's space. For not fitting into my airplane seat. For needing special accommodations for my size and illness. For being the last runner up the hill.

I spent my first year of running apologizing left and right. Uh, hello! Look at me, 280 pounds and literally shuffling along in a 10K and trying not to die. I didn't belong in this world of runners. I just knew someone wanted to tell me that but didn't have the guts. Make no mistake, I was giving 100-percent effort every single time I put on my running shoes. But I knew I didn't look like any of the others at the event.

My reaction? The one I've used my entire life? Apologize profusely before anyone can point out the obvious. This self-defense mechanism fired like a freaking machine gun.

I went on my very first trail run with my friend Josh Gum. No one before had ever asked me to run with them. He and his wife Wendie not only have their own fantastic story about finding a new healthy common path; they both want everyone to learn to love being active outside and love trail running like they do. They have been in my shoes. Josh said he would run or hike or walk or do whatever I was capable of on that day. For some odd reason, I just trusted that he was telling me the truth. I was nervous as hell. During the first few months I found time to run with him, I apologized all over the place. He would run ahead at times, and I would catch up and apologize for making him wait. He would stay with me for bits, and we would chat and tell jokes as I hammered him with questions about running, trails, food, and lifestyle changes. And chafing. Good lord, we talked a lot about chafing.

I would routinely apologize for holding him back from running faster. Or for sucking wind, as I just tried to hang on and run a little bit farther. He would not let me quit. He would tell me stories, or sometimes we would just run in companionable silence. When I could finally breathe again, I would apologize for being so slow. At one point, Josh tired of telling me to stop apologizing. He told me, gently yet firmly, he was done listening to me apologize for giving my all as I learned to run. I needed to knock it off—for my own good. I walked away and really thought about what Josh had said. I still think about that short, hard-hitting, conversation. One of these days, I must ask him about it. I figure he thought that I would work the apologizing out of my system with some confidence and experience in running. When he realized it was just a bad, self-deprecating habit that didn't belong in my life, or in the new lifestyle I was building, he cared enough to call me out on it. And I trusted him enough to listen.

No doubt, you will run into competitive, mean, snobby, impatient, whiny, defensive, judgmental folks in your journey to make activity a solid part of your life. To be fair, we run into jerks in all walks of life. People like me are so hyper-tuned to it, especially as it relates to our bodies and running and sweating, because we feel so horribly vulnerable. As strong and smart people, we fight and persevere through interpersonal obstacles multiple times a day, in all areas of our lives, and don't even look back. But jerks do exist. Just don't go running with them a second time. You will also be blessed beyond measure with some amazing, strong, fun and funny, wise and kind people on this journey to health! Keep your eyes wide open. There are lots of good people out there who will support, encourage, and nudge you along when you need it the most.

A Meltdown

And in case you think I'm immune to comparisons or that I don't battle it routinely … I went on a group trail recently and had a meltdown.

This trail-running group is advertised as being very welcoming. Its members encourage anyone to join them. Those whom I know, including Spencer, are fast and strong and experienced. So it was with trepidation that I joined this 90-minute run, which I had honestly been artfully and purposefully dodging for more than a year. Can I keep up? I wondered. Am I fit enough? The answer turned out to be no. I really couldn't keep up. I got dropped on the first set of hills. I spent the next hour and a half wishing I hadn't, momentarily, been stupidly brave enough to give this a try.

I spent that time listening to some shitty voices in my head telling me I was slow and worthless and a burden. I was questioning my fitness and training. I spent the entire run dreading the moment I'd be last to arrive at the top of the trail, at the top of the hill, or at the parking lot where everyone would be waiting for me. I felt like I was in over my head. I was mortified. Instead of enjoying the company, the scenery and the privilege of spending time running on a glorious early spring evening in Oregon's McDonald-Dunn Forest, I was beating the crap out of myself.

This whole meltdown was about my lack of self-confidence in the world of running. This was about trusting the process that I was working through, in establishing this still-new-to-me lifestyle of careful eating, running, and maintaining my weight. I run with some baggage.

The group had to wait for me in three places. And there is nothing that embarrasses me more quickly or completely than having a group of runners wait for me. I hadn't run more than fifteen minutes before I was flustered, negative, and quiet. I seriously thought about asking Spencer to give me the keys to the car so I could just wait there. Having to explain to him, and to the other people waiting for me at the trailhead, that I was quitting because I felt over my head seemed like a far worse option than just gutting out the run.

We'd carpooled over to the run, mostly so I couldn't chicken out and pull a no-show. On the car ride there, Spencer reminded me multiple times that the other runners were only concerned about their own runs. That they were not thinking about me at all, let alone that I was "worthless," or "a burden," or that having to wait for me meant anything other than following a code of trail running that assures everyone who goes out on a run comes back in. No judgment, only safety.

So back from the run, I made very quick goodbyes at the finish to the few runners who were still around. I jumped in the car with Spencer, but I wasn't going to tell him anything about what I had experienced. I really didn't have the words to express my feelings at this point. We'd gotten to know each other pretty well. And I suck at poker. He asked how things had gone. My intended stoicism flew out the window. I lost it. I attempted to tell him what I'd been feeling the entire run. "I hate being last!" I exploded, among other strongly worded, emotionally laden, self-judgmental crap. "I'm so fucking slow!" I was attempting to process it all through the debilitating fog of shame and embarrassment. Why were the voices, the ones zinging around in my head, so freaking nasty? I would never, ever say those words to another human being. Ever. And yet, piling it on myself seemed like the right thing to do.

I went for a run later that week, still in a funk and feeling bothered, and got some really good thinking time in. I considered how disproportionate my reaction had been to the reality of the situation. What the hell is wrong with me? I wondered. And why is it such a trigger for me to have a group of friends and fellow runners waiting for me? By the time I got home from running that day, I had narrowed down a part of what I was sure was eating at me. I needed to talk about it. "I think all of this stems from me just wanting to be "normal," I told Spencer. "And not to be in a spotlight, for at least once in my life." I lost weight and reclaimed my health in large part to become "normal," something I didn't identify with before. I want to be able to fit in an airplane seat. I want to be able to buy clothes, anywhere, any time. I want to not need medicine. I don't want to be personally noticed for any reason unless I speak up, wear funky clothes, or do something that warrants attention.

Running is a big part of that "normal" equation for me. Even though I choose to run really long distances that most people don't understand, it's all a critical part of helping me to attain a "normal," healthy, sustainable lifestyle. I explained to Spencer that when I'm the last person in on a run, I have everyone's attention. It may be casual, fleeting, and non-judgmental, but for that split second, I am the focus of attention as I arrive to a waiting group. And in my mind—because it's hinging on my body, my weight, my ability, my fitness—I feel incredibly vulnerable. If I were thinner, faster or a better runner, they wouldn't be waiting for me. We'd be waiting for someone else ...

It's a fierce, instant trigger. And now, I think I'm beginning to understand why. Running has become my most beloved health tool, my safe haven in my constantly changing lifestyle. It's the place where I get to be me. All of me. No one but me. It's the place where I can build myself into the person I want to be. No one else but me can do the work, take the credit or see the rewards. So running is about a whole lot more than just the physical act of running. Spencer understands that I want to be a faster, stronger runner. In light of this meltdown, he asked if my goal had changed. No. The goal has not changed. I am finally able to put some words around the reasons why I want to run faster. I don't want to be faster to beat anyone. I'm not competitive. I don't care about getting on a podium. It isn't to shorten a race, or to spend less time running. It isn't because I want to be seen as a better athlete, a better runner, a better person. I want to run faster so I can beat the race cutoffs and finish a race when everyone else in the middle of the pack finishes. I want to be faster so I'm not the last person across the finish line, not the last person to the top of the hill. I want to run "normally" so I don't stand out for all the wrong reasons.

Regardless of my motivation, the goal remains the same. The work I must do to get there also remains the same. It took some serious mental gymnastics to conclude that what I really want is to just be normal, be average. As Spencer continually reminds me, this is part of the process. I just want to be normal.

4 CHAPTER FOUR
FOOD FOR THOUGHT

The whole lifestyle shift upon which I embarked became a black-and-white, life-or-death issue for me. I purposefully kept my thinking along those lines. It wasn't confidence that drove me; it was fear and blind bravery. I got busy discovering and tearing apart some of my basic issues. I was finally getting honest about why I was obese, so that I could figure out how to solve the issue once and for all. In the past, I always responded by placating my wounded soul and emotions with food. Food was how I managed, how I buried shame. Food was my stalwart comfort and companion during these episodes.

The difference now, no matter what strikes me emotionally, is that I do not reach for food as the first impulse. I breathe. I go for a walk. I talk to a friend. I listen to some music. I meditate. I think about why I'm reacting. I do lots of things to soothe my soul, gather up my confidence, and let shame walk right back out the door. I have been careful to build a tool kit of coping mechanisms that doesn't involve food. This is a key habit that I have to keep strengthening and practicing. There is no hiding 399 pounds. When I was obese, I sometimes felt as though my weight issue was open for public discussion just because people could see it.

I recently had a discussion with a group of women at a conference I was attending. We were talking about the comments and helpful remarks that others, including loved ones, make. We all agreed that comments made about food, diabetes, and weight—whether made pointedly or not—simply fuel shame, fears, and lack of confidence. This stuff hurts. And we, the obese, have no real way to hide. Because people can see our bulk, we seem to be fair game for comments and criticism and remarks. It's one of the last publicly accepted shamings and stigmas. It's an emotionally vicious cycle for the recipient:

"Can't you just eat less?"

"You'll never get married, date, be happy if you don't lose weight."

"Should you be eating that?"

"Don't you love your family enough to be healthy?"

I remember exactly who made those comments to me and when they happened. With clarity. I recall how I burned with shame for days and weeks after. I remember how my self-confidence would hit bottom and start digging an even deeper hole. These comments may have been mean, thoughtless, careless, or just plain rude. Yet to be totally honest, I was thinking those exact same things about myself. When you own a thought and someone says it out loud, shame comes barreling through the door, with cake in hand.

I still wrestle with food, weight shame, and confidence issues. At some point, though, my attitude changed. Shame no longer drove what I did or what I did not do. It was still there, for sure, but I could shut it up for periods of time. I was ready to change, to change everything. I knew things could be totally different than they were. I knew it was time for excruciatingly lonely, hard work. Every other emotion or fear or thought, even shame, was edged out by that intense readiness.

A Way of Eating

A woman who hadn't seen me in a while walked up to me during an after-work reception and said, "I'm just going to follow you around and watch what you eat. I need to lose some weight. Maybe I can learn from you."

Nothing makes me more self-conscious than knowing someone is watching or judging what I eat. I spent a lifetime trying to hide the true bulk of what I was consuming. And I got really good at making sure no single person had the whole picture. I mean, c'mon. I was wearing my poor eating habits for the whole world to see. And I had pretty solidly convinced myself I was hiding things well enough to deflect attention. Insecurities run deep and old habits die hard. Even now, I'll still find ways to skip social events that involve food, if at all possible.

Throw into this particular awkward party mix that I'd just done a long run. What could that possibly have to do with food? I had burned over 1,000 calories running that morning, and I was freaking hungry. I was eating anything and everything that was not nailed down. And someone wanted to watch me eat? Egad! I promised this woman that I would share what I used to eat, compared to what I eat now—and she promised to stop following me around.

From my late 20's to early 40's, on any given day, I was consuming roughly 4,000 to 5,000 calories of mostly fast food, carbohydrates, and highly processed foods. I was not exercising. A typical day looked like this:

- Breakfast: McDonald's sausage biscuit, hash browns, Diet Coke

- Snack: Chips, large Diet Dr. Pepper

- Lunch: Qdoba nachos (loaded), large Diet Coke

- Snack: Candy or more chips, large Diet Dr. Pepper

- Pre-dinner snack: Two McDonald's cheeseburgers, large fries, large Diet Coke

- Dinner: Chicken enchilada casserole, rice and beans, chips and salsa

- Bedtime snack: Ben & Jerry's Phish Food ice cream

It's unbelievable that someone could eat that poorly, that volume of food, isn't it? I wish I were making this up ... but I really did eat all that stuff. Daily. I have witnesses. Hell, I have proof. My weight and diabetes diagnosis are confirmation that this was pretty typical fare for me, for years. You don't just suddenly wake up fat.

Starting in the early 2000s, with my diabetes diagnosis, I spent about eight years settling into a diabetic diet. Portions got smaller. I worked to cut out refined and overt sugar. I focused on a lower-carb diet with healthy fats. I lost about 85 pounds during this time period, and increased my walking over the years. I wasn't perfect, but it was a huge improvement.

July 2011 rolled around, and I decided I was going to build a new and different lifestyle. I wanted to be healthy. And a whole lot of additional changes, beyond food, have happened.

So what does my eating look like now? I tend to eat low carbs with healthy fats. Even the standard American Diabetes Association promoted diet is too high carb for my post-diabetes, metabolically compromised system. There are arguments that it's too high for most diabetics, actually. So, taking personal control of the situation, I learned that the trade-off to stay off of medicine is that I use food to control my insulin/glucose. I consume about 1,500 to 2,100 calories a day, depending on what kind of exercise I'm doing. I work out six days a week.

A typical day for me now looks sort of like this:

- Eggs with veggies scrambled for breakfast and sometimes for dinner too.

- Nuts, celery, nut butters, fresh berries, cheese, small portions of lean meats for snacks.

- Lunch and dinner are often lean meats with lots of veggies, in bowls or salads.

Just a few short years ago, I would tell everyone that I hated vegetables and couldn't imagine life without Diet Dr. Pepper. Things have changed. And I remember the day I texted my friend Wade with the epiphany that, hey! I *liked* veggies. He immediately called me, laughing. I think he said something about hell freezing over. We now share veggie recipes. You don't just suddenly wake up healthy. You actually have to work pretty hard to get here.

Apples for Apples

Here's a piece of advice for chronic dieters who really want to be successful in changing the way they relate to food: learn what true hunger feels like. I was brutally honest with myself when I started this journey. I knew I had a big problem: a really unhealthy relationship with food. I've mentioned that later on this journey I would be diagnosed with BED and it would answer so, so many questions. But early on I was winging it and making up the rules as I went along. And early on this journey I had figured one thing out; I was going to stabilize blood sugars, get off insulin, lose weight, and try to find answers to complicated food issues, all at the same time.

My biggest hurdle was that I fundamentally did not understand hunger. My body had not been hungry in years. Years. I didn't know the feeling. I was so used to simply eating because it was mealtime, or because I passed the fridge, or because food was in front of me, or because it was a special occasion, or I was sad, or … I'm not alone. In any conversation with folks who have lots to lose, the conversation at some point will come around to hunger, and to the ways we ignore it, abuse it, refuse to allow it to happen.

I had to figure out what it meant to be hungry if I was ever going to get a handle on overeating. I was pretty sure that the only way to have long-term success would be to feel and understand hunger, and respond appropriately to that hunger. So I came up with a trick that would (a) teach me to understand hunger, and (b) wouldn't mess too badly with my blood sugar.

The trick? Apples. Fresh, crisp, cold apples. I put a bucket of apples in the fridge. And I made a deal with myself: anytime I thought I was hungry — when it didn't make sense for me to be hungry (as when I had just eaten lunch or had consumed most of my calories for the day) — I could eat an apple. And only an apple. If I were indeed hungry enough to eat an apple, then I was probably legitimately hungry. If I was not hungry enough to eat an apple, then I was not truly hungry — I was simply cruising for food out of habit or boredom or emotions. I used apples to train myself to at least stop and recognize whether I was experiencing true hunger.

The worst day? I ate six apples. I had days when I just couldn't tell if I was hungry or mentally craving food, comfort, or company. So I ate apples, burden-free, guilt-free. I was trying to teach myself to learn something new, so I gave myself permission to eat as many apples as I needed.

And boy, did I eat a lot of apples in those first few months.

Just this week, I had to buy another big ol' bag of apples and put it front and center in the fridge, just to remind me to listen to my hunger. Just to remind me not to eat because I'm bored or tired or lazy or frustrated. I don't think any of us are ever done learning. And those of us with food issues are never off the hook. We must stay vigilant about not letting bad behaviors creep back in. That's why that big bag of apples is in my fridge. I find it ironic and fun that while we give apples to teachers as gifts, in this case, apples have been my teachers.

Farewell to Sweets

I am not on a diet. I am not being punished. I am simply and willingly making dietary choices based upon what works best for me. This is a way of eating. I have banned candy from my life because of my complete lack of self-control. I am not one of those humans blessed with the skill of moderation. Eat one cookie? A bite of a candy bar? One small slice of pizza? Yeah, right. I'm an all-or-nothing kind of girl. That's really good stuff to know about yourself.

Yet I have had people, quite literally, get in my face about my food choices. The harshest comments are usually triggered when I choose not to eat something. "Your diet would kill me." "Your life has to be so boring if you can't even eat cake!" And my favorite (not), "Just one bite is not going to kill you!" You get the idea.

Here are a few things I do when I feel confronted or questioned about my food choices:

- Walk away.

- Find a friend who knows my story and stand with them. Because I still lack confidence in my relationship with food, I seek out friends for comfort. Maybe it's not a healthy trade-off, but it works for me as I gain confidence.

- Decline invitations if I know my food choices will be scrutinized, or that my decision to not eat will be taken poorly or cause problems for the host.

- Just take a portion of whatever is being adamantly pushed on me and quietly get rid of it out of their eye shot.

I'm working hard to make the choices that are best for me, and for sustaining my healthy lifestyle. The process is non-stop learning. The biggest hurdle for me continues to be accepting that not everyone needs to approve of what I do or of the choices I make. I am learning to resist the urge to apologize, explain, or defend my choices to everyone. I am not asking anyone else to buy into this crazy, neurotic food ride that I am on. It works for me, and for me alone.

The one comment that always puts me on the defensive is the "one bite" comment. People seriously tap into the deepest of my emotional injuries with that. They don't even realize it: one bite could kill me. Perhaps not literally today, but when I was managing diabetes and battling obesity, food was a very real, dangerous, controlling drug for me. With very real implications that showed up on a blood glucose monitor or a blood test. When I was trying to establish strong new habits, one bite could lead to a real mental and emotional unraveling, down a very steep and slippery slope. I knew it. One bite could be the difference between winning and losing a battle. Or between winning and losing the entire war. Why? Because that is what had always happened to me in the past. Having that one bite was not about being flexible or daring or easygoing or accommodating. For me, that one bite was entirely about the act of giving up and giving in. One bite leads to two. And that is exactly how I wound up at 399 pounds at age 42. I'd lost the battle countless times. I knew the one-bite battle all too well.

I have had to work hard to reframe my entire relationship with food. It's one of the parts that's not overtly visible, unless you eat with me often, you read my food journals, or I've chosen to confide in you. So that's about three people. Seriously.

This is how I choose to view food today:

- Food is fuel. I treat food as a means to fuel my life and my goals.

- I focus only on eating when I am physically "belly" hungry.

I had to move away from thinking about food as comfort, peace, solace, friendship. That's what it had been for most of my life. When I was in the throes of battling diabetes, I had to also move away from thinking of food as poison or adversarial. It's been constant, private, diligent efforts. And I'm not done. Not by a longshot. Am I really saying there are certain foods I'll never eat again? For me, yes. That is my choice and it works. I think some of my struggles and battles with food choices may resonate with a handful of folks. I don't believe that my all-or-nothing tactics would work for everyone. I would never actively encourage folks to follow in my exact footsteps. Everyone has to find his or her own path to health. Make your own choices. Discover what works for you.

Nourishing Snacks

These days, I don't go anywhere without having a snack handy; it keeps my new lifestyle habits cemented and in focus. I can be relied upon to dig up a snack from my purse, a pocket in my gym bag, or the stash I keep in my desk at work. There's an apple, a healthy snack bar of some kind, a small bag of nuts ...

This is a habit I learned as a diabetic. If a "low" hit — and it often did — I had to be able to help myself. When I was on a pharmacy of medications, there was no real way to predict when a low would hit. I always had something ready to go that was glucose-based: a juice box, glucose tablets, candy. Snack-carrying was simply about blood-glucose manipulation and management. It was basically another form of medicine.

It took only one time of heading fast into a low blood sugar episode (light headed, nauseous, foggy thinking), and not having glucose to help myself stop the rapid downward spiral, for carrying a snack to become an ironclad habit. Imagine stealing a handful of sugar packets from Starbucks and rushing into the bathroom, slumping to the dirty floor to eat them as fast as possible ...yeah.

Today I carry snacks for an entirely different reason. Maintaining my weight and my healthy eating habits requires me to keep a certain level of commitment, to make sure I have what I need, to keep practicing the good habits. Holiday parties? An extra-long commute home after a busy day? Endless meetings at work? I think we all get caught in situations where we get hungry and our options for healthy foods are limited.

Carrying snacks isn't just about healthy eating. This new habit is also about battling a really old, profoundly strong and unhealthy habit: making excuses. I was really, really good at making excuses. If I don't plan ahead and prepare for those times when I'm hungry, I'm forced to rely upon others or on surrounding circumstances. For me, that became a built-in excuse for eating like crap. A license to go wild. Permission to just eat whatever happened to be available. It was an excuse. Not packing a snack to help myself manage my food and life goals was simply a big, fat excuse. Carrying a snack removes that excuse.

At one point in my life, when I was flying weekly for work, I used that excuse all the time. I saw every trip to the airport, and every day spent away from home on a business trip, as an excuse to eat whatever I wanted. This was an adventure and a "special occasion," after all! Weekly. I traveled weekly. It's no wonder I weighed 399 pounds.

So now, I pack snacks. It's a cross between a hobby, an obsession and self-defense. I take it very seriously. I don't want to lose my foothold in, and passion for, this new, healthy lifestyle. It's a pretty simple and easy trick. It's decidedly unsexy and boring, but it works for me. Having a healthy snack within arm's reach removes excuses. It keeps me in control. It helps me to stay focused daily on my food, weight, and lifestyle goals. When I pack my bag for the day, I make sure I have some kind of snack stashed away. I don't leave the house without going through a mental checklist: wallet, keys, lipstick, snack...

Here's what you can usually find in my purse, car, desk, or gym bag: apple, 150 to 220-calorie bar of some sort with no added sugars (Kind, Epic, Quest, and Picky bars are some favorites), piece of string cheese, and a small bag of mixed nuts.

Cinnamon Gum

How do I get through the holidays and not gain weight? I create and stick to a simple, straightforward plan. I follow that plan to the best of my ability.

- Activity. I am going for a run. I will work up a sweat. No, I am not exercising so I can eat more. I am exercising to be healthy and live a balanced life. Exercise is a habit and a choice. I don't skip it just because it's a holiday.

- I wear snug clothes, bordering on uncomfortably tight, to the feast. I'm not going to feel like overeating if my pants are already cutting me in half.

- I take along foods I know I want to eat, and that fit with my food lifestyle.

- I engage in good conversations, games, or any positive distraction. It should never be all about food.

- I keep a favorite flavored water on hand.

- I eat a normal breakfast.

- I load my plate with veggies and salad, and fill up on that first.

- This is not the only meal of the day, not the only meal of the year. It's not as if I couldn't get or make any of this stuff, any time. I don't let perceived specialness lure me into eating more than I intended.

- I eat fruit for dessert.

- And when I'm done eating, but am tempted to graze? I chew sugar-free cinnamon gum. It kills the taste buds. I chew a *lot* of cinnamon gum.

There's nothing earth-shattering in my plan. These are probably all things you've heard before. Having a plan and sticking to it is really the point. And having a pack of cinnamon gum.

Don't forget the gum.

Red-Flag Holidays

The Christmas holiday season, from Thanksgiving through the New Year, (or even Halloween to the Super Bowl in some of my social circles) brings an entirely new set of challenges to the table — so to speak. Most people agree this is a season of feasting. Let's talk about the special set of coping skills you might need to protect your new lifestyle from family, friends, or feasts.

This is a dangerous time of year for me. Some of my favorite foods start appearing in stores and at holiday parties. They're seasonal foods, which to my mind means they are scarce and treasured and not-to-be-missed. In most cases, these crazy wonderful delicious treats are tied to some of my happiest childhood memories. I know I'm not alone.

I was shopping with my sister, Deb, when we suddenly found ourselves in the candy, food, and gift aisle. You could smell the sugar floating in the air. Deb held up a package of something, "Do you remember this?" Fancy cookie mixes. Almond Roca. Peppermint anything. Chocolate everything. Fancy drink mixes. Maple candies. Candy canes. *Candy canes!* You get the idea.

I replied, "Yes!"

The conversation going on in my head was not so simple. A pair of fat little devils were sitting on opposite shoulders, whispering in my ears, "You could eat that and just go run it off, and you wouldn't even have to give up other foods today in exchange. You don't have to tell anyone." "Actually, you're at a stable weight, Bets. You did just run a really big race. I mean, c'mon! You earned this! You could eat this and totally get away with it and get back on track tomorrow." "It's the holidays! Celebrate! Why are you so freaking strict with yourself? It's just a piece of candy!" Red flags everywhere.

That's not the kind of healthy thinking I've been working to develop. I fight these cravings, habits, and impulses all the time. I'd be lying if I said I didn't have to think about it every day, holiday or not. I've been thinking this way for over 40 years. It's still kind of the default. It's oddly, sadly, disturbingly comforting.

Early in my journey to gain control of my lifestyle, I had to handle things by simply not being around things. So I didn't go anywhere near specialty or holiday food aisles. I avoided parties and potlucks. I couldn't walk through the bakery section at Costco. I avoided weddings and showers and parties. I brought my own food to family dinners. I was very, very careful to limit just how hard I would have to test my resolve. Stark? Severe? Yes. I knew I needed some distance and some solid practice in creating new habits around food to combat the old ones. I needed time to get practiced and strong. I knew it instinctively, defensively, so I was really careful. I was extra restrictive for several years. And at times, I still choose to be restrictive about social settings that involve food. I'm only human—but I'm a human who loves her current life and wants to keep it that way.

5 CHAPTER FIVE
THE COMPARISON TRAP

The daily grind can easily erode away confidence, or stop you in your tracks if you have to battle it too many times. It sucks. So, let's just talk about some of it and quit pretending that it doesn't exist. This is the stuff I battle intently, intensely, and consistently. This is also the exact listing of where I was derailed in every past attempt I made on a diet or exercise regimen.

- I would not talk with anyone about my fat rolls, my bulk and weight, and the problems they were causing when I tried to exercise. Chafing, motion control, infections, back strains—I suffered in embarrassed and humiliated silence for a very long time. I was deeply ashamed of my bulk.

- Life felt unfair. I was going to bed hungry, feeling overwhelmed and alone. I often felt pissed off that "normal" people could eat whatever they wanted. Meanwhile, I was a freaking air fern that could gain weight by merely smelling cookies baking.

- Diabetes. I was trying to get off insulin, yet having to add more back in. There were the endless finger sticks; the lows that made me an unbearable, cranky, bratty turd; the commitment to eating the right things at the right times and not be over calories for the day. Relentless attention to food and medicine.

- I was so sore from exercise I literally thought something was broken or damaged.

- I excused myself from social events. If I went, I chose not to eat what everyone else was eating, then tried hard not to look awkward, or sad, or out of sorts.

- I avoided chronic food pushers and saboteurs like they had the plague.

- I hated not seeing results. I could restrict calories, yet the scale wouldn't move for days or weeks. I would walk farther, but not find it any easier. I would do the same things as my friends, who were having success, but not achieve my own weight-loss goals.

- I wanted to quit. I felt overwhelmed knowing there was no end in sight, ever. These habits had to be "for life."

- All my food had to be measured and counted. I exercised every single day and drank plenty of water. I maintained good blood sugars. I did everything I was supposed to do — and the scale said I was up! Aargh!

- The scale dictated my mood and feelings of success. I would become a thundercloud of despair because I was up half a pound on any given day.

- I would revert to comfortable habits when the rest of my life was out of control. I would cheat on my own rules, then panic because I knew this behavior would only drag me backwards.

"Every day is a new day," my friend Wendie told me. "You have to start over every single day, no matter how hard it is, you fight through it and you start fresh the next day."

Judging

Talk of fairness usually leads to discussions about the ugly, damaged side of its family tree: comparison. I think they're twins. A sense of unfairness was an obstacle that I often fought. I would go to bed, stalk the seasonal candy aisle at the store, or leave a food-centric event feeling as though things were unfair. It was a tough burden to carry every single day. I would then replay, over and over in my head, choices I was forced to make. What I'd eat and not eat for the sake of weight loss and blood sugar control. What did I give up? What could others eat? It seemed things just weren't fair when they were eating pie, cake, pizza, or anything chocolate, seemingly without consequence, and I had to actively avoid them.

I realize that this is me judging others for their choices. I understand the hypocrisy. Even that stark realization never seemed to stop the "fairness" bus from taking a few laps around my brain. It turns out that a mind-set of unfairness doesn't serve anyone well in a fight for a new lifestyle. Instead of tackling the real problem and finding a way to change things, my mind was fully engaged in futilely figuring out what was not fair; how to make it fair; and how to justify things, with side trips to the land of "shortcuts," "cheats," and "substitutions." This thinking was getting me nowhere.

On second thought, it was getting me somewhere. It was getting me upset, disgruntled, unhappy, and just a little bit pissy. It also encouraged pouty, whiny, self-defeating thinking. I realized that it translated into the negative crap that falls out of my mouth when I talk about how I see myself. I was wicked-sharp, lightning-fast, and brutal with my comparisons. When I took the time to tear apart my thinking and my resulting behaviors, I was inevitably led to the conclusion that no good would come from these comparisons. I knew that it was not fun to be around someone who felt, and talked, as if life was unfair, or who constantly compared themselves to others.

So, some years ago, I decided to work on a few things. The hard, sad, ugly things just had to be fixed if I was ever going to have a shot at reclaiming my health. I would have to confront the things that weren't helping me, the bad habits and self-defeating behaviors. My issue with food was just one of the big things I would have to face. Another big, nasty issue was comparing myself to others. It emerged as one of the top three challenges I would have to confront, along with food and my ongoing war of self-hate of my body and abilities. What are my core issues with comparisons and fairness? I'm still working on identifying all of them.

I realize that I play the self-defeating comparison game when I am low on self-confidence, battling for self-control, embarrassed, exhausted, or fighting jealousy.

Comparison. Lord, it's evil stuff. These are some of my thoughts:

- She is thinner (or she runs faster, she can do more, she has a better body, etc.).

- He can eat whatever he wants with no worries.

- They're losing weight faster than I am.

- He was blessed with good genes.

- She doesn't even have to work to be thin.

- They don't have to watch every single bite they eat.

- Why is no one else suffering? Hungry? Sad? Angry?

- They aren't struggling with a disease — like diabetes — on top of dieting.

Now and again, I still fall into the trap of comparison, and the feeling that fairness is in short supply. I still fall into comparison more often than I would like. And I know that I am not alone on that one. The important thing now is that I'm more likely to catch myself and stop.

Just stop.

I want to be happy with just being me. I want to be comfortable in my own skin. I want to love what I have and not yearn for what I don't have. I want to focus on what I can do and what I get to do.

I remind myself that I have one life to live, that no one else gets to live this exact life. Comparison usually phases into overwhelming gratitude. Thoughts of unfairness eventually give way to wholehearted appreciation for the embarrassment of riches I have in this life that I am really just starting to live. There is no comparison for that.

As President Theodore Roosevelt once wrote: "Comparison is the thief of joy."

On Not Giving Up

I look back on some of my early journal entries from this lifestyle makeover and wonder how in hell I made it to today. Honestly. Why didn't I just quit? It was brutal at times. I understand the "How did you not give up?" question perhaps better than any other single inquiry. I don't have a good answer. I mean, I had quit every other time I tried to start exercising to lose weight. I really am only now succeeding for the very first time.

Check out these journal entries:

1/10/2012. I tried step aerobics class. I didn't understand the routines and can't physically keep up. I stood behind my step and marched in place for 45 minutes. Drenched in sweat, red-faced, and couldn't breathe from working so hard. It was humiliating. I walked out to my car crying. I feel ashamed and embarrassed.

The very next day: *1/11/2012. Today was the first day of circuit weights. I am five hours post-lifting, and I am so sore, I can't lift my arms. I could only do about a fifth of the workout. Maybe less. I can't bend, my fat belly is yet again in the way. Everyone in there has been doing this for years, and I'm intimidated to hell and back.*

84

How and why did I keep going? Why didn't I just return to my old, easy, comfortable ways?

My journal records those first sad, too-honest, desperate entries. Yet in the following weeks, I'm only documenting glucose readings and weight, noting that my appetite was through the roof. There is curiously nothing else about why or how I continued with aerobics, weights classes, walking, or learning to run. Nothing.

When I'm asked how I kept going when things were tough, I usually answer with something basic but true: I wanted my life to be different. I was sick and tired of being sick and tired, and I was ready to do the work. And I knew that what I was doing was hard. So I just did it. Those sound like platitudes or motivational quotes. But that was really, truly how I felt. Fiercely, totally, with all my heart. I was not giving up this time, no matter how hard it got. I knew there was a different life that could be mine.

I had promised myself I would do what I had to do this time around to get healthy, be fit, and to create a whole new lifestyle. This time around was not yet another one-fix wonder, a silver bullet, a starvation plan. I, the chronically impatient, knew I had to be patient, because I was trying to exchange prescription drugs for food and exercise. I had to invest the time and effort to build something I could keep and do for the rest of my life.

When I think about it, even before I committed to trying to change my lifestyle, I was often hungry, sore, and defeated — because I was fat, sick, and totally out of shape. I mean, I was taking three shots a day, handfuls of prescription meds, and I was carrying anywhere from 100 to 220 pounds of extra weight most of my adult life. That required a substantial amount of work in and of itself. So, really, the whole "hungry, tired, and sore" thing hadn't changed. It was no longer a valid excuse for me to use. I think my brain and heart recognized the equation of wanting to fight for my health, and that needing to find a long-term, permanent solution was the only way to make this happen. I was finally choosing to listen to the little fire in my soul that was screaming, "Things can be so, so different for you if you'll just work at it!" At long last, I could hear it loud and clear.

The biggest mystery for me in my whole crazy adventure is why I finally chose to listen to that little voice, which I'd smothered for so very long. And I work every day on making that voice stronger and louder.

Dealing with Shame

When people talk to me about my story, they seem to identify with my sense of shame more than anything else. Indeed, shame was right smack-dab, in the middle of my own lifelong struggle. Shame made me feel as though I had to work harder and fight harder than a thin person to be considered worthy. Shame made me feel like I had to apologize to the world for allowing my overweight existence to intrude into their thin world. Shame convinced me that most conversations about my worth and professional abilities probably went like this: "Well, she's good at her job ... for a fat woman." Shame had me questioning whether anyone, beyond my immediate family, could ever love me. I may have seemed normal on the outside, yet on the inside I felt as if I were being eaten alive by shame. Shame manifested itself within me as I tried to eat myself to death.

Here's how a couple of esteemed researchers and psychologists describe the emotion:

"Shame is the intensely painful feeling or experience of believing that we are flawed, and therefore unworthy of love and belonging," wrote Dr. Brené Brown.

"Unlike guilt, which is the feeling of doing something wrong, shame is the feeling of being something wrong," said Dr. Marilyn Sorensen.

I wore visible proof, every single day, that reinforced the public perception that I couldn't control food and I was lazy. So I ate to bury the embarrassment and pain and shame.

Now, however, I actively work to put shame in the past tense. I am rarely in that place any longer. And I catch it a whole lot quicker. I am not asking for sympathy, not trying to sound sad or desperate. Public presentations I make with Novo Veritas, my consulting business, demonstrate that I was never alone. They show me that a lot of people, both men and women, are weighed down with shame, even paralyzed by it. Weight, bodies, food habits, past failures — the list is long and emotionally daunting.

It turns out that vulnerability can be a very powerful ally in fighting shame. "If we share our story with someone who responds with empathy and understanding, shame can't survive," Dr. Brown wrote in *Daring Greatly*.

When I began to put the feelings and reasons for my shame into words, something amazing started to happen. Shame no longer had me in a chokehold. I chose to have soul-baring conversations with people who knew me, who cared deeply about me, and whom I trusted. I talked my way into a whole new experience of freedom when I opened up about the things I was ashamed of. I talked about hating my body. I talked about developing a deadly disease due entirely to my lack of control over food, and my laziness. I talked about embarrassing, mortifying, horrible moments. I talked about being lonely and alone and unlovable. I talked about the physical indignities of being so obese that I literally could not care for my own feet.

There was some pretty deep shame involved in my story. It turns out, it's a lot of the same shameful stuff that other overweight people have in their stories, too. While shame is largely in my past, I admit I still have moments of doubt and shame and fear. Who doesn't? I've been able to figure out at least two of the major triggers that cause me to revert to old ways of thinking.

Shame seems most able to rent temporary space in my head when (1) I'm tired or (2) I'm trying something new that scares, frustrates, or embarrasses me. Discovering these basic triggers became a major weapon for me. Now, when I'm feeling pain or sadness or heartbreak over not belonging, I know I'm more than likely just tired. And I'm not flawed and worthless and unlovable because I'm trying to learn a new skill, or can't yet quite do what everyone else can do. I'm more than likely just scared or embarrassed. Knowing the triggers gives me a better chance at changing the self-dialogue in my head. That dialogue is so different than it used to be. Am I cured? No. Are there times I question my worth, or whether I'm lovable? Hell, yes.

The key now is that I can usually recognize and stop that line of thinking, much sooner rather than later. And even if shame grabs a temporary foothold, it no longer sends me looking for the answer in the kitchen, the candy bowl, or a fast-food restaurant. Exposing shame to the light is the only way you can begin to fight it.

Fat Shaming

Fat shaming started early for me. Middle school and high school were, predictably, the worst.

One day during my junior year, I walked out to my car in the high-school parking lot. Someone had pasted a bumper sticker on my car that read "No Fat Chicks," with the "No" removed. I was being called a "Fat Chick." I had suspected that people thought it. This removed all doubt. I was a farm girl in the middle of Los Angeles, and I was fat. I was an outcast on so, so, so many levels.

My farm-girl side had some practical tools. I pulled some silver duct tape out of my glove compartment and covered the bumper sticker. A carful of high school boys passed, laughing and pointing and taunting. I knew them all. When I got home, my mom helped me scrape it off my car. We were both in tears. We never told anyone.

To this day, the thought of this incident can still make me cry if I think about it long enough. Then, the tears were for the cruel act and confirmation that I didn't belong. Now, the tears are of sadness for my mom — for the fact that she's gone, coupled with my deep gratitude and love for that woman, who understood what it meant to be unacceptably large in our society.

Psychology Today defines fat shaming as "an act of bullying, singling out, discriminating, or making fun of a fat person. The shaming may be performed under the guise of helping the person who is overweight/obese to realize they need to lose weight or they will die, become ill, and/or never succeed in life or relationships. Fat shaming is an individual bias against people who are considered unattractive, stupid, lazy, or lacking self-control."

I have many stories of my own. I also hear them from a surprisingly wide variety of both men and women—when they choose to be vulnerable and relate their stories. They try to be casual and funny. They're not. They try to tell me it was parental "love." It's not. They try to tell me they deserved to be the butt of a cruel joke. They didn't. They try to tell me they're over it, that they've dealt with it. Then their faces crumple. You can't just unhear the things that have been said about you. I have tried and tried and tried.

Fat shaming is about both actions and words. They are equally devastating. The actions range from elbowing someone's fat rolls if they sit next to you on a plane, not hiring someone for a job because you don't like how they look, or making animal sounds as they walk past. As for words, they can rattle around the receiver's brain for years. That old childhood rhyme—"Sticks and stones may break my bones, but words will never hurt me"—is utter bullshit. Words create. They wound. They can build and fill your heart with joy. They can also destroy. Words matter deeply. Don't let anyone tell you otherwise.

Beware the Scale

I had always allowed a number on a machine to tell me if I was "good" or "bad."

Here is what I wrote to a woman who told me she was upset over gaining back a pound after days of solid, diligent work:

"Quit stepping onto the scale more than once a week. Yes, the scale gives us feedback — but it can also lie. It does not take into account everything that's going on, nor does it address all of the other areas in which we've made great progress. It's a number. A snapshot. A moment in time. The bottom line in this lifelong healthy adventure is that we move and feel strong and eat as wisely as we can. Period. The scale will follow or settle or do whatever in the heck it's going to do, but we are not going to be ruled by it. I would love for you to be healthy and happy and not give a damn about a number on a scale. That number tells absolutely nothing about the fabulous and amazing young woman you really are. And just for the record, the irony in me telling you this is that I struggle with the scale every day. This is my fight, too."

During one particular six-week period following a 50K race, my weight struggle was abnormally intense. I found the scale slowly climbing. It was perilously close to the top end of the range that I set for myself. And it was climbing even though I was doing what I knew normally worked. I was feeling fat and lazy and sluggish because I was in rest-and-recovery mode. Although I knew better, I began watching the scale, waiting for it to stop going up. Spencer reassured me. Josh and Wendie told me stories about it. I read articles. The people I trusted and loved all basically said, "Chill. This is normal."

Given my history, I was deathly afraid this was not normal. I was sure this was the first step toward my regaining every single one of those 200-plus pounds that I had lost. That idea, that fear, was totally consuming my brain. I had experience in being fat. I did not yet have experience in maintaining a loss or stopping a gain. We got back to training on January 2. I was eating solidly, within my calories for the day. And the scale was still creeping up. Finally, I decided it was time to panic. I thought that was a perfectly reasonable reaction.

I told my friend Taryn Hand, a registered dietitian, about my concerns and what I was doing to try to stop the climbing numbers. The look on her face grew increasingly troubled as I described my habits: I weighed myself daily, sometimes up to three times a day. I'd hide my scale from myself—then I would unhide it, step on it, and hide it again. In my own house. I felt anxious. Constantly. One day, the scale was much higher than I thought it should've been. I felt like crying or throwing up. I felt totally out of control. I thought my heart would explode from my chest. I knew it was a ridiculous physical response. I wear a heart-rate monitor when I run. Out of curiosity, I put it on to see if I was imagining all of this. In a resting or non-active state, my numbers range anywhere from 45 to around 70. When I am running easily and comfortably, and can chat with friends, it ranges from about 125 to the 140s. As I was panicking about the stupid number on the scale, my heart rate was 132. My heart was working as if I were running, but I was standing perfectly still, in the middle of my bedroom.

I needed help. Luckily for me, Taryn staged an intervention. She didn't realize how perfect her timing was. She told me to stuff my scale in a bag, put it in the trunk of the car, and hand it over. "Do not weigh anymore!" Of course, I stepped on it the night before, and the morning of, in total defiance. My last two little data points on this roller coaster. I hauled it to Taryn and handed it over. She has given me good advice on ways to collect feedback, to judge progress, that don't rely on a scale. The one that ultimately worked best for me was noticing if my pants started to fit snugly. She has been talking to me about this stuff all along. But suddenly I was a motivated listener. For a long time, Taryn hung onto my scale. I weighed in with her every other week. I didn't look at the number: She just told me if I was within the range we had agreed upon.

You want the ugly stuff that's part of the behind-the-scenes on this journey? Welcome to my fight with the scale. This is what freedom from the scale looks like to me:

- I now weigh once a month to make sure I'm in range.

- I eat healthy and track what I eat.

- I stay active.

- If my favorite pair of pants get snug, I will go back to the eating plan that helped me lose weight in the first place, until my pants fit comfortably again.

In retrospect, had I kept an open mind when I started my journey, if I could have listened to and absorbed some grounded advice, what would have been helpful? These are some of the things I really wish I could have told myself about the scale and numbers:

- Your weight fluctuates. Daily. It can go up or down during training, on your period, if you eat too much salt, with the rotation of the earth.

- Understand that your weight is not stable from day to day. It isn't going to happen. Quit thinking that's even possible. You thought you got to a number and stayed there with just a little effort? That this whole body-weight thing was simple math, cut and dried? Uh, hell no.

- Don't pick a number for a goal. Don't pick a clothing size, either. Pick a feeling, an activity, an ability, a destination. You want to climb stairs and not have to gulp for air. You want to feel good about how you feel in your bathing suit or your birthday suit. You want to be able to hike, run, walk, or move better. Pick something that isn't a transient, essentially meaningless number!

- Take measurements. I really wish I had known how big my hips, belly or thighs were at my largest. I didn't take measurements because—hell!— who wants to know they have a 75-inch waist? But you will wish you had those body measurements for reference and reassurance in the process. At any point when you're feeling "fat," stalled or just wondering how far your journey has taken you, you can pull out a tape measure and be assured, well beyond the confines of a simple scale, that you weren't gaining anything but muscle and fitness.

- Worry is wasted energy. Spend time looking for solutions, progress, and opportunities.

- For the love of all that is holy, quit beating yourself up! You, at the very core of your being, are not the same as the packaging of your body or the number on a scale. You may not grasp what I'm trying to tell you—but please, please, just believe me on this one. I realize this is probably the last thing you can wrap your mind around when you've battled your weight your entire life and a scary number is staring you in the face, a number so big you didn't know the scale went that high. I know the feeling of panicked desperation and hopelessness as well as I know the sound of my own heart beating. Reach out to me (my contact information is in the back of this book) and I will relentlessly remind you of your value to our world. I'm a way better judge of your value than a stupid mechanical piece of crap you bought at Costco.

- Do not let that scale dictate your mood to the world. If the number is up a bit, do something about it. Don't be a bitch, or walk around like someone ran over your dog, or take it out on your loved ones. Don't start secluding yourself from the people you care about, because you feel you don't deserve their love, or you're deeply embarrassed. Stop allowing that stupid scale to alter your mood.

- Know that the big picture is worth all the little steps—all the missteps, concerns, questions, and sacrifices. It's hard, mundane, relentless work. It's worth it. And this is in no way linear. There is nothing direct, straight, or logical about the path you are on. You're going to be making stuff up as you go.

- Love on yourself and believe in yourself. You can't see the day when you will be healthy and happy, but it's coming. Your weight should not be allowed to dictate any of that. You have so much to offer the world. You're a mother, a daughter, a sister, an aunt, a friend. You are a unique blend of a lot of really remarkable things that no one else in the entire world can possibly be. We were only given one of you. Do whatever you can each day to help yourself get healthy, so you can be around and enjoy the life in front of you.

- This isn't a short-term investment. Every day, you will look at something and judge it as not moving, as failing, as plateaued. If you can just hang on and look at this as a 365-day investment, you will see growth. Keep at it. You didn't gain weight overnight. You will not lose it overnight.

One of my favorite songs of all time is Tim McGraw's "Live Like You Were Dying." I was living this weight-loss journey with a lot of fear. I feared failure, judgment, going backwards. The fear that I have embraced, that I live with, could choke an elephant. What if I could just enjoy the journey for what it is, live each day as if I were trying to be my very best? Living like you're dying doesn't mean you live with no consequences for your choices. It means you accept each day, for what it is, and keep moving toward the goal you want to reach.

A Fake Belly Button

Skin is elastic, but not that elastic, especially when it has been stretched out for more than 20 years. When you lose a lot of weight (200-plus pounds, in my case), you wind up with excess skin. In my case, it was almost all belly skin. It turns out that this is actually a big problem, and not just aesthetically.

My belly flap of skin hung to the top of my thighs. Loose skin develops its own inertia, which means I had to become an expert in compression gear if I wanted to do anything other than stand upright or walk casually. This meant tank tops, shorts, girdles, ACE Bandages, Spanx, you name it. It was a daily task to figure out how to stay active while keeping the loose skin from hurting me. I was developing arthritis in my spine from the skin that pulled on my lower back. I had chronic infections and abrasions on the loose skin of my belly. I tried every potion, cream, and gizmo I could, in hopes that the skin would magically shrink back.

Finally, my sister directed me to a cosmetic surgeon. He gently told me that nothing would make the skin retract. The only cure was removal, and the surgery was a tough one. It was not covered by insurance, even though I had documented back issues and chronic skin problems (Insurance did wind up covering part of it, when the surgeon uncovered three significant abdominal hernias during surgery.). I talked with my family and friends to make sure they were supportive.

I saved every penny. I talked with other patients who had done the surgery. I asked Spencer to help me get as fit as possible, which I knew supported good healing and a faster recovery. So we set up a marathon-training plan. And the target marathon was surgery day. I prepped for the surgery just like I would have a race.

On November 20, 2013, I had a procedure called a "full-body lift." It was an eight-hour surgery. I have a 360-degree scar around my waist at the "bikini" line. Nearly ten pounds of excess skin was removed and my abdominal wall was rebuilt as part of the surgery. Basically, all the skin covering my ribs, upper abdomen, waist, and back got pulled down tight. I had more than 1,000 stitches in my abdominal wall, which now has four vertical "pleats." The circumference of my hip line had internal stitches; the incision was glued externally. I lost my belly button, which I find highly amusing. I told the doctor I didn't care if I had a navel, but he said I needed one or I would look like a "Who" from Dr. Seuss's Whoville. So he built me a fake belly button. It's an innie!

For several post-op weeks, I had three closed-suction drains on the incision line that pulled excess fluid from the surgical site. It was as uncomfortable and hard to manage as you might imagine. And because my abdominal wall had been reconstructed, I was leaning forward perpetually because it was stitched tightly. I had to learn to stand up straight again and not be hunched over. I used the word "Ouch!" a lot, often paired with a cuss word. It was a great day when the drains were pulled out. In the doctor's words, I was healing from "massive tissue trauma and disruption." Uh. Yeah. That's one way to describe it.

Before surgery, I wore size 16 pants to accommodate the extra skin. The day after surgery, I was in a size 12 despite swelling, drains, and a surgical girdle.

To be honest, in the early phases of healing from this surgery, I was sure I'd made a horrible, terrible mistake. It was simply a brutal experience. There's no other way to describe it. I had never had to deal with that level of pain. Immediately after the surgery, I may have texted a few friends, asking them to come kill me. I'm glad none of them listened.

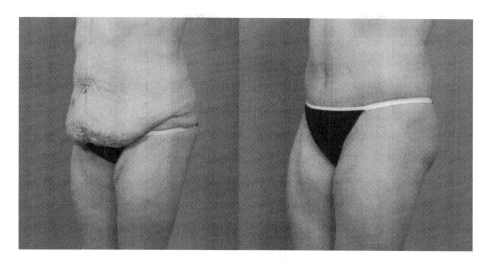

Pre-surgery picture November, 2013. Post-surgery picture April, 2014. With a fake belly button, ten pounds of skin removed, the abdominal wall rebuilt and the 360-degree scar hidden by the elastic of the bikini. It was the best solution to get rid of the loose skin, chronic infections in the skin folds, and a disintegrating lower spine. (Used with permission by Timothy Connall M.D.)

This surgery has a high complication rate. It is known for a prolonged and difficult recovery because of the 360-degree incision. I had an almost-flawless recovery. There were a few minor surface infections, but nothing major. The doctor kept telling me this was because of my healthy diet and perfectly controlled blood sugar, and because I had taken the time to get in shape for the surgery. I avoided all the major complications. And the surgery was well worth it.

One of my goals from this surgery was to be able to throw on a sports bra and shorts, and just go run. Previously, I could not begin to imagine that kind of freedom. Now, without excess skin, I didn't have to worry about compression gear, infections, belly-flap chafing, and my own extra skin beating me to death.

The summer after my recovery, Wendie and Josh invited me to go to Bend, Oregon with them to run. Wendie knew about my heartfelt goal of running in just my sports bra, no matter how silly. We chose a fabulous stretch of trail at Tumalo Falls (which, ironically, are now my home trails!) … two-and-a-half hours from Corvallis, so we wouldn't see anyone we knew. About 45 minutes into the run, I finally got brave, and hot and sweaty enough, to take off my shirt. I may have cried. Just a little. It was an incredible feeling to run with nothing but the basics, just because I could. Today, my fake belly button and I are free to just grab my favorite running clothes and a pair of shoes, and go run anywhere, anytime.

It's a dream come true. This surgery changed my life.

Josh and Wendie Gum, "The Sports-Bra Run," Tumalo Falls, Bend Oregon. 2014.

Mental Gymnastics

The late, great baseball player, Yogi Berra, once reportedly said, "Baseball is 90 percent mental. The other half is physical."

Forgiving Yogi's arithmetic, he could have said the same about running. More than once, I have found myself in a big-time battle with my brain. And it has handed me more than a few ass-whoopings.

Recently, I had a run that left me feeling profoundly humiliated and sad. And I let it get to me. The more time I spent sorting this out, the more I realized it was not about the specific details. Not at all. It was entirely about how I reacted, about the things I allowed my brain to latch onto, and about the things I kept telling myself that just weren't helpful or even true. My next couple of runs after the "incident" were horrible. I would run a little, then stop and cry. Run a little, then walk in a tantrum. Run totally pissed off at myself, then stumble along crying in anger. In those moments, I was oddly grateful that I run trail. At least there were no human witnesses. I kept playing a mental recording of things that were mean, uncharitable, and nasty. I was listening to them intently. I was crying. A lot. That reaction alone was bewildering and confusing to me.

I found an opportunity to have lunch with my friend Ana Lu, a compassionate and unfailingly optimistic woman. She's a trail runner and a sassy Latina who is brilliant in her ability to bridge communities together. I want to be Ana Lu when I grow up. One of the fun things about our friendship is that she is a non-native English speaker who, while she speaks fluent English, loves learning and incorporating American slang into her vocabulary.

And man, oh man, have we had some hilarious moments with me trying to explain certain phrases and words. Imagine being on the mats in the gym, which happened to be on a college campus, trying to hold a plank position when she says she heard some college students talking and wanted to know "What's the difference in 'nailed,' 'screwed,' and 'hammered?'" I and everyone around me collapsed into heaps of laughter.

Over lunch, I told her about my experience, the process, the aftermath, and some of my conclusions of this bad running experience. I asked what she did when she found herself in a state of emotional turmoil. She suggested I build myself a "life raft" — which resonated with me. She told me to write myself a love letter, call a friend, meditate, run in my favorite spot, read positive stories, write in my journal, run with good friends who wouldn't question my silence or tears, buy new music, post a huge note on my wall declaring my next goal, all to keep me focused and excited. She told me that when I felt like crying in the middle of a run, I should just stop and cry my heart out, holding nothing back. To get it out of my system, no matter who might be watching. Any one of these ideas, she said, could be my "life raft."

Ana Lu also told me that I should write about all of this — and not just because of the running aspect. No one, she argued, really talks openly about this side of the lifestyle-change process. It took about three more days for me to realize that running was simply the trigger for this emotional drama. A conversation with Spencer really helped me begin to recognize and understand what was going on. Ana Lu saw it, too. She gently called me on it. It wasn't about running at all. It was about self-doubt. Fear. Lack of confidence. Shame. A distorted body image. It was about work that needed to be done to help my brain catch up with where I'd taken my body and my life.

Maintaining and cementing a new lifestyle is, statistically, harder than losing weight. I had always thought people were full of crap when they said losing weight was the easy part. Losing 200 pounds and reversing diabetes was hard work, relentless and scary. I read somewhere that less than five percent of people who lose weight actually keep it off. Statistics show that once someone reaches their goal weight they're likely to bask in the glow of achievement for a while, then quietly and slowly relapse into old habits. Maintaining lifestyle changes is not the norm.

And now? Now that I'm at a solid weight, eating healthy, staying active, and focused on keeping my weight in a consistent range, it turns out those who have been down this path really were *not* full of it after all. It's all hard. So, now what? Now that I have reached my goals of losing 200 pounds and banishing diabetes and learning to run and be active ... what next? Now, I continue the hard work of hanging onto my lifestyle changes. And continuing to learn and adjust to what works for me and my body, day in and day out. Along the way, I continue to diligently jettison the old crap as I find it. I just have to keep working to help my brain catch up with where I'm at. Oh, and by the way — I now have an emergency life raft cobbled together. It's anchored close by, and ready to go for the next run.

Sticks and Stones

For a trail runner, sticks and stones are common foes. My friend Josh calls me "Princess Face Plant," a nickname I've earned for good reason. I'm fortunate that, for me personally, no serious mishaps have transpired—though I will admit there have been some close calls. I have friends who have met worse fates, from broken bones to career-ending injuries to my friend Rita stepping perilously close to a coiled rattlesnake on a trail. Tripping, falling, and blood are typical of what we take on when we hit the trails.

On my run today, as I really began thinking about it, I realized some of the worst wounds are inflicted not by sticks and stones, but by words. Sometimes, words said to me and others I know have been imminently hurtful. Oftentimes, it's from a person who has no clue they've lobbed something upsetting in our direction. Comments on my weight, or on how my body looks, send me into a tailspin every time. "Aren't you too big to be a runner?" is the one I can't seem to forget. And I've done a ton of work to try to get past this issue. Then I found a great blog, *The Critique of the Female Trail Runner*, and realized I'm so not alone. Writing on Gina Lucrezi's www.trailsisters.net, Sandi Nypaver detailed some of the rude and mean things that are said to and about some of the wildly talented, elite female athletes in ultrarunning. I can't stop thinking about it.

The issue isn't just about running. We have probably all dealt with negative comments, thoughtless words, and rude treatment. And I know from conversations with my guy friends, this isn't limited to women. There is a whole lot that you can't see or know about any individual person, and commenting just makes things worse for them.

We can all pretty much agree that these days, cowards and bullies hide behind social media to say things they would never say to someone's face. Telling someone she looks "too thin" isn't going to help her on her road to recovery from anorexia. Telling me that you "didn't know women my size could run" is not helpful to me in maintaining my weight and my commitment to fitness. Telling my friend, who is recovering from a serious accident, that he looks "scrawny and weak" is not a confidence-builder on his road to restoring his fitness and stamina.

None of us knows the full story of another's struggles. We really don't know about their passions, their desires, their personal fights, and back stories. So often, we take one look at the physical shell and make a judgment based upon how someone looks. That's not helpful or kind. Shouldn't we really endeavor—in this harsh, tough world—to help and encourage others and show them kindness when we can? It's really pretty simple.

Humiliation

One of my fears did play out early in my gym-going experience. It's a humiliating story, but I share it because the episode wound up providing me with clarity and motivation. I had been working out for about a month. I probably weighed 325-plus. Two guys were on the mats near me. One guy stage whispered to his friend, "Dude, why is she even trying? It's not like it's gonna to make a difference." I froze. I was the only other person around. They were talking about me. I was wounded. Mortified. I tried hard not to cry. I failed. I laid on the mats and wept as soon as they walked away. It stung deeply for at least a week. My worst fear had been confirmed. People were mocking me. But eventually, it made me mad and more determined.

When I stopped to really think about it, I had already seen progress in the four short weeks I had been going to the gym. Almost every other person had been nice to me. My blood sugars were better than they had ever been. My pants were fitting more loosely. I could walk more laps on the track. I belonged in that gym as much as those derisive idiots. As much as anyone. I may have been fat, but they were jackasses. I'm now healthy, but I'll bet that guy is still a mean jerk. The rest of my gym experiences were routine.

Don't get me wrong—the work was and still is hard. Learning was scary. I sweat a lot. I had some physical challenges. I still felt totally intimidated. But the fears rattling around in my head were all just that — in my head. If I stood staring at a machine, I was asked if I needed help. No one cared that I was fat and in their space.

The very first time I went to the gym, I walked into the locker room with my gym bag, looking as though I was either going to cry or bolt — or both. A woman saw my distress, waved at me and said, "Hey, do you need help finding your locker? I did when I started here." She assumed I belonged. She offered help and was friendly. There wasn't a hint of judgment. She instantly smashed to smithereens some of my long-held fears. It cost her nothing to be kind. I valued it deeply.

I've had bad moments, met mean people, had pointed comments aimed at me. The truth is, there are mean, ignorant people in the world, well beyond the walls of a gym. Are you going to let them stop you? Have I felt dumb and ill-equipped and out of my league? Hell, yes. I have fallen off a stationary bicycle. Twice. This is where having a sense of humor and being able to laugh at yourself is key. I have wanted to quit more times than I can count. But I was determined to win this war against obesity and diabetes. I've made friends who hold me accountable and expected me to show up. Having friends and staying focused on your goal are essential to the not-quitting process.

Forgiveness

When I was young, my friends, relatives, and most of the responsible adults around me just turned a blind eye; I was urged to "lose weight" so the "mean comments" would stop.

I remember one instance where anyone pushed back on a bully on my behalf, when my sister, fists balled up and standing on her toes, told one of our neighborhood bullies to shut his mouth — and she was about a quarter his size. Forty-plus years later, I can still clearly picture her incensed little face and feel the sisterly love from that moment.

It can be hard to accept social media friend requests from people who once said hurtful things I still remember more than 35 years later. I accept their requests because the only way to change the tide is for me to forgive, and to do what I can to make things different, not only for myself, but for others, as we move forward.

You can't embrace your future when you're clinging to bitterness lodged in your past. You name it, I have a story that relates to being embarrassed, belittled, made fun of, hurt. Workplace. Dating. Stores. Restaurants. Travel. And before someone suggests it, these were not times when I was being overly sensitive or reading too much into something. These were pointed comments and situations that were clearly aimed at me being fat in their space — of people trying to "save me" or simply "stating the obvious."

I would bet good money that most of you reading this have stories you could also share. I also have stories that came after I lost a lot of weight, of people who made comments to assure me they like me much better now. In and of itself, this is another form of emotional upset: "You're pretty now!" "Why are you still single?" "You must love your life now!"

I've been diving into this topic with both feet, trying to learn what can be done to change the tide, and to learn how to help other men and women who struggle. Fat is not the only thing that's shamed. With help from the media, anything we deem "not normal" or "not acceptable" is fair game, right? As I was formerly a 399-pound woman, fat shaming is where my heart and brain lie. I can talk about what it was like being morbidly obese in the U.S. and now, no longer being obese, I can talk about both. And I do. All the time. It's not as if you can hide being obese. It's not as if I was obese to piss anyone off, or to make myself a target. There were some really complicated dynamics behind my weight, as is true with anyone. Being shamed for it never drove me to do anything other than eat, hide, and cry. It never provoked the need to change, only to try to hide and to avoid people. I think we have to start somewhere.

This is a list of the best advice I have gleaned from my tumble down the rabbit hole of books, internet, podcasts, and experts on fat shaming and bullying:

- Be kind to yourself. The worst, most destructive, most hateful fat shaming is the shaming we do to ourselves.

- Shut down other people when they say mean things about themselves or other people.

- Support the positive.

- Stop commenting on anyone's food and clothing choices, or on how their body looks.

- Comment upon and praise actions, abilities, and character rather than appearance.

- Don't repost, like, or comment on any mean shit on social media. It's not funny.

- Don't assume. I don't know the next person's journey. I don't know why they eat a certain way, what challenges they face, what health conditions exist in their lives. I take one breath, one moment, to adjust my thinking: I don't know what's best for them, or what might hurt them.

- Taste your words before you spit them out.

- Use your powers for good.

Words with Friends

"I can't eat that! It's not on my diet!"

As soon as you utter those words, someone will instantly search for a way to "help" you get around the "can't."

"Can't" means restrictions, deprivations. It means something is unfair, or that you must be unhappy. "Can't" is a signal word that others respond to, usually in a negative or sympathetic way. They want to fight for you, convince you otherwise, remove the barrier. It provokes all sorts of responses that reinforce the negative response that I had just put out: "I couldn't do your diet!" "Just one bite won't hurt." I even got an, "Ugh. Your life sucks." My friend Wade encourages me to approach it from a different angle. "Quit saying you can't," he says. "Quit saying it's a diet. It's not. It's a lifestyle. It's a choice. Quit feeling like you must defend your choices to everyone. It's none of their business."

One of my biggest *aha*! moments came when I finally heard what Wade had been telling me. I started practicing and learning how not to defend or explain. I worked on believing in, and stating, my choices. By intentionally choosing different words to talk about my relationship with food, I began helping others understand that I wasn't being defensive.

Words. Who knew?

My close friend Liz gave me much the same advice. She's my lifelong cheerleader, a butt-kick-when-I-need-it kind of confidante. Everyone should be lucky enough to have a Liz. I was telling her that people weren't as supportive of my life choices as I had hoped. She said, "You chose this. You know you can do it. You don't have to ask for permission. You don't have to defend what you choose to do to anyone." Wade and Liz were right. Dodging social invitations or avoiding my friends wasn't sustainable. Relying on other people to support me, or to be okay with what I was doing, wasn't the answer, either. This was all me. It was my fight, my life, my choices. And when I really got to thinking about it, the core issue was actually pretty simple: I needed to start by changing my language.

If I changed how I talked about my choices—food, diabetes, exercise, all of it!—perhaps I could set people up to respond more positively to what I was doing. So I tested it out. I started saying:

"I choose not to eat that right now, but thank you."

Funny. Nobody really seemed to argue with me when I said it was my own choice. I mean, they might argue, but they seemed less likely to argue than when I was proclaiming unhappy absolutes. Most folks will instinctively argue against a restriction. Life shouldn't just be about "I can't" or "I don't get to ..."

When you alert folks that this is a choice, they usually respond accordingly. I choose. I get to. I want to. I found that people overwhelmingly responded with support when I stated things in the positive. They may come back with something like, "Okay! It's over here if you change your mind." Or, "Can I get you something else?" The conversation is totally different. They don't pressure me. They don't fight my choice. They don't try to convince me otherwise. They seem to simply respect that I am doing what I want to do. Talking in the positive does some amazing things to one's thinking, as well. I have better resolve. A better attitude. I am more persistent and stubborn. All of that has continued to get stronger since I changed the way I talk about my choices.

It's a subtle and simple resolution that takes some practice. Take charge of your words. Make them positive and strong. People will respond by supporting you. And best of all? Your brain will follow. As we cement lifestyle changes, it's really our brain that we have to convince—and keep babysitting.

"Whether you think you can or you think you can't, you're right." —Henry Ford

Friendships that Work

Relationships get stressed and tested when we make sweeping lifestyle changes. I know this is not news. Our friends can help and support us, and be our biggest fans. They can also challenge us and sometimes hurt us. Fractures in friendships are serious, heart-wrenching stuff, especially if they occur during a time when we are actively trying to create changes and to make things better for ourselves. I get questions from people angry and upset with friends. Friends who tease their children with candy and junk food; friends who express jealousy at their weight loss success; friends who try to sabotage their eating plan; friends who make mean remarks about why they eat or don't eat certain foods.

This kind of thing often happens to those who have made significant lifestyle changes. Perceptions and interactions with friends change as our life changes to shift the balance. The learning curve involves everyone. Some handle it better than others. You might sit there shaking your head, but you have done this kind of crap to your own friends when they were succeeding at something and you were not. We somehow feel threatened by someone else's success or determination or bravery. We have all done some version, subtle or overt, of not supporting a friend who is in the grip of a lifestyle change. We have all been *that* friend at some point, no matter how hard we tried not to be.

People can be mean, especially when they are hurt, cornered, scared, defeated, embarrassed, or jealous. Those who know us are often the most capable of inflicting deep wounds. I try to remember that meanness may come from a place of hurt, which is damn near impossible to remember when you are the target. Meanness is actually about them, not about you or me.

When it comes to forging a new, healthy path, you might find yourself having to draw a line in the sand (or having to build a brick wall!) to protect yourself and what you're working toward. Even with friends. The growth, death, or transformation of friendships is very much a natural part of all the change that occurs, the change that we create with a major lifestyle overhaul. We can grasp intellectually that change is going to happen in our lives. Understanding and accepting all of the dynamics involved in changing friendships, as they play out in real time in our lives, is a whole different story. I still have many of my same friends. Honestly, I discovered several of my valued relationships were based heavily on and around food. We have since found other ways to value, grow, and enjoy our friendships.

I am blessed to have a small handful of close friends who are actively a part of this never- ending journey. Some are old, some new. All of them, with no exceptions, are 100 percent supportive of the new lifestyle I have built. It's a tight and intimate circle of friends. Some old friends are no longer a part of my life. The relationships simply and quietly went away, for a variety of reasons. We drifted apart. We just let it happen. And that may simply be a natural product of life and have nothing to do with a changing lifestyle. A few friends said mean things, were openly not supportive, or were creating problems. Actions and words spoke loud and clear. The offshoot was tough conversations and a purposeful severing of contact. I struggled hard with handling the friendship-ending issues. I don't take friendships for granted, or throw them away. I want to protect and preserve friendships to the greatest extent possible. The conclusion I finally reached was that, to preserve the friendship in each of those cases, I would have to sacrifice—in some way, shape, or form—what I was trying to do to reclaim my health. Their inability or lack of willingness to embrace my changing lifestyle actually helped me to make the hard decision; it was more important to have my health than any particular friendship.

I have more than my fair share of stalwart and solid friends who have been on this crazy adventure with me. I lucked out. I know it. They're doing the hard work right beside me. They coached me through eating one serving of dark chocolate (not the whole bar) the first time I ventured out to try adding chocolate into my diet after three-and-a-half years. They have guarded the bushes and trails when I jump off the path to, um, get close with nature. They meet me at the trailhead to run in the rain, or at the gym at o'dark:30 to lift weights with smiles on their faces. They find places to eat that make food choices easy for me, and they enjoy it as much as I do. They remind me of where I was a year, two years, five years ago ... and not-at-all-gently remind me to stop comparing anything to anyone other than my old self.

Those actions speak so loudly, you can't even hear the words. All along, my heart has belonged to this tribe that seems as committed to my success as I am. They're my friends. I'm lucky to have them. They have made all the difference in my world.

Just Breathe

I remember calling my friend Wade about a year into this journey, when I hit a really rough patch. I told him I'd been faithful to my regimen for weeks on end, eaten perfectly, exercised daily, yet I'd gained weight. Pissed-off despair would be an accurate description of my emotional state. He had seen it several times. His job was to talk me back onto solid ground.

Wade listened patiently for a bit, then said something like this: "You're not doing this just for today. You know that. Your work will show up on the scale next week, or the week after, if you keep at it. And maybe the weight gain is just because you need to shit."

And then his trademark … "Breathe, Bets. Just breathe."

I have the benefit of some distance and perspective. Without a doubt, I have a certain amount of selective memory about this whole lifestyle journey I've been on. I know that. When I think about why I hung in when things got crappy (pun intended), it was largely because I had some strategies I used to get through the rough and trying times. I was focused on reversing diabetes. That was the driving force.

Sometimes you just need something smaller, something you can get your hands and mind around, when you are overwhelmed with chasing down a really big goal. These strategies work most of the time (not all of the time!) to keep me focused and motivated on some level. I think they're worth suggesting just in case one of them happens to work for someone else:

- Incentives and trade-offs. What would you do with a handful of cash that you did not spend on fast food? Would you buy a new jacket or running shoes? Would you go somewhere fun? Knowing I was trading McDonald's for the Maui Oceanfront Marathon worked for me.

- Goals. Once I signed up for my first race event, I was not going to waste the money by being unprepared. Signing up for an event gives me something inspiring and fun to focus on. Taking the additional step of telling some friends ups the accountability factor.

- Phone a friend, one who has permission to be honest with you, who knows about your journey within the context of your life. The right friend can remind you that you might just need to poop to solve all of your problems.

- Look (briefly) to your past. Take stock of where you are versus where you have been. We typically do not see the subtle, daily, positive changes. Sometimes it's an old photo that will provide the gentle visual nudge you need. Before, during, and after pictures remind me that even if I am not yet where I want to be, I've still made undeniable, positive progress.

Incentives, goals, strategies, trusted friends. I know that none of this is new. They are all time-tested tactics. And they work.

Wade and me at Pacific Crest Endurance Festival. I talked Wade into doing this triathlon with me, then three months prior to the event I chickened out on the swim. I did the long-course duathlon, he did the long-course triathlon. He gave me tons of grief about it, which led to me eventually taking swim lessons...

6 CHAPTER SIX
ULTRA-CHALLENGED

So, why do I run? I mean, that's the question that started this mini-revolution within my larger lifestyle change and has led to a crap-ton of self-discovery.

I spent the past summer thinking a whole lot about running. I was injured and couldn't run for about eight months. At one point around July, four months or so in on the injury, I just wanted out of pain with this stupid hamstring attachment tear and a medial collateral ligament (MCL) tear. I realized I genuinely didn't care if I couldn't ever run again and that kind of shocked me. It was that forced distance from running that would allow me to really begin to see the individual trees in the forest more clearly. In the category of perfect timing, although it felt like a life-train derailment, this down time with a running injury was also around the time I began intensive work with a therapist to dive deep into self-confidence and my relationship with food and my body. It was a perfect storm, occurring at the moment I was ready to do the work, that forced me to get pretty honest about *why*. Digging into the whys of running led me straight into some raw and scarred ground that was long overdue to explore.

Thankfully, my relationship with running has grown up along the way. I have to admit, even though it hurts, I started running as an act of self-punishment. I was beyond pissed at myself for being fat, unhappy, unlovable, miserable, and lonely. As a fat woman, the act of running physically and mentally hurt and felt shameful, obscene, and embarrassing; it was perfect punishment for the misery I'd created. So, so much twisted self-hatred in the beginning and at other times along the way. I didn't see it that way at the time of course, and I *never* uttered any of this thinking out loud to anyone. *Ever*. I just thought I was running to try to lose weight. I never examined the emotions or motive. Admitting all of that to myself allowed me to see running, my history with running, and myself in a very different light.

Therapy has helped open the door for me to embrace running as a tool and not as a weapon. And my relationship with running is not linear or stagnant. I don't think anyone's relationship with running is. It went from punishment to elation to goal-driven to meditative to rewarding. Sometimes all in the same run. But regardless of why I got started or how I stayed connected to running, it's changed me. Running became a big part of my healing and discovery and my life.

So then the next question is … uh … they have 5Ks … Why the hell did you pick ultras?

Stick with me for a moment. I love this sport, race day or any day, because it tests the individual. It's absolutely about individual effort. Yet in a strange way, it's almost like a team sport. And I think this is so important to understand. I struggle with belonging on so many levels. And this sport feels like a welcoming community, one I've never felt before. If you can see that, you can begin to understand why the ultrarunning world drew my heart, legs, and lungs right into its midst. It's partially about doing something extraordinary. Something totally outside of the box that houses my comfort zone. No doubt it was about pushing boundaries and trying to see exactly what I was made of. It's also, for me, deeply about the community of people who can support others' dreams and hopes and goals while they pursue their own. I've always loved this quote by Erica Cook: "I'm not interested in competing with anyone. I hope we all make it." Nowhere in my life is this quote more alive than in the trail and ultra world.

We all genuinely want everyone else to "win" their personal race, no matter how they define it. No matter what their finish line looks like. If they are fighting their heart and guts out to lay down their best effort, we're rooting for them. Period.

Here's where the community piece emerges: I can name professionals and elites I've seen waiting at the finish line, many hours after their own finish, cheering on runners. I've seen other runners, crew, and volunteers flying into collective problem solving to keep another runner patched together and running. Imagine coming around the corner at mile 27, which is in the middle of the course with no one else around, and seeing that the race winner from the previous year (kind of a big deal in our running world!) is there giving everyone — every single runner still on the course — high fives and words of encouragement. Or imagine the voices of other runners echoing through the hills as they all pause their own races to ask, "Are you okay? Do you need help?" when they encounter another runner stopped on the side of the road. When one runner comes across another struggling to keep moving forward, it's common to buddy up to walk or run with them a bit and encourage them along the same stretch of trail. We run as individuals. No one else can do the work to get us to that finish line. We all seem to understand and appreciate that and genuinely support that — which is where this strong community knits at the most unlikely seams and shows itself.

What did it take to get ready for that first ultra? I ran a whole lot of shorter races for a year trying to learn the ropes and build endurance and confidence. Most of the races were simply practice to get me to a point where I could run an ultra. That is where my sights were set.

Running an ultra — that's 50 kilometers, or 31 miles, and beyond — was something I'd been thinking about for three years. My friend Josh Gum had planted the idea in my head a long time ago: "You do not have to run fast," he said. "You just have to run far." I'm never going to be speedy. I know that. But … stubbornly refusing to give up, once I set my mind on something? Really? That is practically my superpower! For most of 2014, I focused on training for an ultra. A trail ultra.

I picked the North Face Endurance Challenge 50K in San Francisco, with jaw-dropping views of the Golden Gate Bridge, as we ran through Stinson Beach and Muir Woods. Hills, mud, redwoods, beaches, the Golden Gate. And I'm a third-generation Californian with a new lease on life; there was something important and sweetly poetic to me about going back to run in a state where I'd only ever been obese.

It was a perfect race. I finished a little sore, hungry, muddy, proud, with a big smile on my face … and totally looking forward to doing another! It felt so good to have been focused on a big goal for a long time, to have done all the hard work day in and day out for months on end, then to finally see it come to life right before my eyes.

I ran the entire race with my friend Jeff Sherman. Like me, he had never before run an ultra. In fact, he was a super late registrant to the race when he realized I was going to be running it alone. He toed the line of his first 50K, and while he was fit and healthy, he had never even run a 10K! He was game, he made me laugh and kept me moving, and I did some of the same for him.

We crossed the finish line together after eight-plus hours of running. I have a selfie of Jeff and me smiling at the 5K mark. We're both all energy and hope and joy at embarking on this epic adventure, and it shows on our faces! At the marathon mark, I took a selfie thinking we would both be smiling, so close to being done! Instead, the epic grimace-with-middle-finger selfie was born. After the race, I would see that it was a picture of me smiling in the front, clueless to Jeff behind me who was letting me know what he thought about the distance we were running. And perhaps telegraphing that he didn't think we were even close to being done. It's one of the best series of pictures ever. Right after I snapped that picture, he said something about me owing him a whole pizza and "a stolen truck of beer." We finished, gathered with all our friends, and went and ate pizza.

And we got Jeff a beer.

So I ran my first ultra and it was everything I imagined it would be. And so much more. Including the next day with delayed onset muscle soreness (DOMS) that is the feature of many hilarious post-running memes with runners avoiding stairs and sudden movements. Hell, I needed assistance getting up and off of the commode because my legs were shot. At least all of my traveling housemates had a good sense of humor and we were all similarly crippled from the previous day's extraordinary athletic endeavors. We all vowed next time to get an Airbnb that didn't have a single stair involved.

I was officially hooked on the world of ultras. I love this sport more every single time I lace up my shoes.

Jeff and me at the 5K mark.

Jeff and me at the marathon mark.

The Longest Mile

Now is probably a pretty good time to tell you that the first mile lies. Big time. The first few minutes do not tell the whole truth. They are not an accurate indicator of what is to come. You soon learn that you must grit your teeth, ignore the lies, and look for a good spot, mentally and physically, to settle into and just get past that first mile or so. Experienced runners understand this. They are merciful enough to pass on this wisdom quickly to any newbies they encounter.

Ask my friend Jeff about that first mile we ran together at the North Face. This normally happy, funny, energetic, and optimistic person was, well, suddenly very not. Alarmingly not. Now, in hindsight and with some time, it's freaking hilarious how not happy he was. I kept encouraging him. "Jeff, the first mile sucks. It will get better. Hang in there. Keep moving." He made some pretty pointed, off-color comments. By mile three, he was finally settling in and ready to kick into high gear. He was no longer cursing. And most notably? He was smiling again.

I got to thinking about this phenomenon the other day during a run (I was comfortably beyond that first mile.). Why, after six years of running six days a week, does that first mile still kinda suck? I am not talking about the entire run. It really is just that "getting started" part of each run that is not to be trusted. Even this morning, on a short and easy run on familiar and favorite terrain, it took me a mile or two to settle in, get into a rhythm, and push aside the naysayers in my brain. It takes me some time to simply battle it out with my legs, brain, and heart, and get all systems to accept that I'm going to run, no matter what other plans they may collectively have. So they should all just shut up and start working together, please and thank you!

You're really wanting to ask me: why do I keep running if it's that hard, each and every time I lace up my shoes and get started? That's a very good question, one I ask myself often. It's because I know how I feel when I've finished running. Not just with a single run, mind you, but with the cumulative habit and lifestyle of running. No matter how poorly I may do in a single day; no matter how much I fight my mind at the start, or how wet, hot, cold, sweaty, grumpy, dirty, or chafed I am; or even if I trip and fall flat on my face — I never, not once, no matter how good or bad or weird or hard the run has been, I never regret running. Running as a habit buys me endurance, health, strength, and pride in myself, and a growing trust in my body's ability to do difficult things. And this doesn't even touch on the other perks that running has added to my life: the friends, scenery, memories, laughter, being outdoors, and the discovery — in my fifties — of the pure joy of being alive and moving. After that first mile or two, I almost always hit a groove or a spot of some comfort with the routine. My mind begins to settle down, my feet get more comfortable finding the earth, and my heart tries to find the sky. The consistent habit of running has very literally saved my life.

Running is hard. Making the time is hard. Fighting through some initial discomfort each time, each day, is hard. No one ever said the good things in life would come easy or be comfortable. And my lifestyle as a runner is far easier than living with obesity and diabetes. Running is just one of several important tools that helps me continue to cement my lifestyle shift. Eating well and being active daily is what, if I am lucky, will keep diabetes away for a few more glucose-stable decades. When that first mile sucks, these are the things I try to remember.

When I turn on my Garmin (GPS tracker) and head out on a run, I use that first mile to remind myself of where I was just a few short, fat, unhealthy years ago. I focus on the result and the reward that I know comes from the process of fighting through that first mile, day in and day out. I think about how hard I have worked to create a new, healthy lifestyle. I think about being handed a bona-fide second chance at living life to the fullest. I think about no longer being diabetic or taking shots or swallowing handfuls of prescription meds. That first mile can lie all it wants. But I don't listen anymore. I'm in this for the long run.

Storm Troopers

On Memorial Day weekend of 2015, I had one of the most epic experiences of my running life — and one of the most terrifying moments. All in the same day.

The Western States Training Camp is an annual three-day gathering of ultrarunners based in Auburn, California, in the foothills of the Sierra Nevada. It's a practice event designed to help runners learn the trails for the Western States Endurance Run, a historic 100-mile trail race — the one that launched our sport! — that happens each year at the end of June. This camp is open to non-racing runners as well. New, veteran, fast, slow, as long as you have a love for the sport and pay the registration fee, you are warmly welcomed. Endurance-running nerds—like me—should really put this well-run, flawlessly supported camp on their bucket lists.

I attended camp with Spencer and our friend Erica. We had all planned big events over the next few months, and this was a great kickoff training weekend. We ran 32 miles on Saturday, 18 on Sunday and 22 on Monday. Big miles, new terrain, new friends. All good. Erica is Australian and a large-animal veterinarian. And one hell of an all-around athlete competing in Ironman Kona. She's tough and funny and supportive.

That's the epic part, including the running companionship. Now to the terrifying.

On the first morning, we were bused up to Robinson Flat, in Tahoe National Forest, to begin a run back to the Foresthill Elementary School. As soon as the buses unloaded, Spencer took off. Erica and I waited in a long, female-exclusive line for the lone pit-toilet before we began our run. We were enjoying one last hint of civilization before being "one with nature" for the rest of the day. There are so many stories I could tell about squatting in poison oak, missing turns, avoiding snakes, gold mines, and pioneer cemeteries. I could talk about doing anything to escape that overly chatty chick from Maryland, including a desire to push her off a cliff. Those are for another day.

At mile 26, Erica and I hit the last aid station at Michigan Bluff. We quickly stocked up on water and food—watermelon for me, peanut butter and jelly for Erica— and took off again for the finish line. Around mile 29, it began to rain in big, wet drops. The weather forecast for the weekend had promised 80 degrees and clear skies. Now it was 55 degrees, raining, and starting to hail. We joked about finding a weather person for a "friendly" conversation about their forecasting skills. And because we were cautious trail runners and in new mountain terrain, we were both carrying waterproof running jackets. But it wasn't just hail, it was thunder and lightning, and it quickly became very, very frightening. A blinding, bright flash of lightning lit up the skies. Holy smoke! We were soaked and cold, halfway between the last aid station—itself a tent with metal poles—and the finish line. We ran on a raised and semi-exposed dirt road with trees on either side and a three-strand barbed-wire fence next to us. There was nowhere to hide. Then more thunder. This time, it seemed to be moving away. Whew! No lightning was visible. We kept moving.

Then, about fifteen minutes later, the storm seemed to double back on itself. Almost simultaneously, we heard a loud thunder clap and were startled with a blinding, bright flash of light that we both insisted was directly over our heads. The thunder was so loud, it numbed our eardrums. Erica and I nervously began to consider our best survival options. We were serious. We were trying to decide how to (a) not freak the other one out and (b) get our butts off the exposed hill and down to the school alive.

We kept moving, after agreeing that if there were another near hit, we would stop to wait out the storm, making ourselves the smallest of possible targets per wilderness safety advice, away from big trees and obvious lightning rods. And that's about the point that the hill crested and we finally wound downhill. On the descent, with the thunderstorm moving away, we came upon a fellow trail runner who was literally hugging a tree. Death grip. Both arms. She was crying. She said she was too scared to go on. She was terrified. Erica calmly and gently convinced her to move away from the tree and follow us down the trail. We couldn't just leave her there. In some strange karmic twist, this was the beyond-annoying "chatty chick" whom we had wanted to push off several earlier cliffs. She still couldn't stop talking. Thankfully, my hearing was temporarily impaired by the thunder. Small blessing. It was the longest ... mile ... ever.

When we finally reached the forest gate and headed for Bath Road, the paved road leading to the school, we encountered several cars checking on runners they knew were still on the hill. Spencer was in one of them. "Do you guys want to get in the car?" he asked. "Or do you want to finish this thing?" Erica and I replied in unison, perhaps a little subdued or resolute sounding: "Finish."

This entire endurance sport is about learning your strengths and boundaries, testing your limits, then finding the mental fortitude to fight beyond all your tiredness and fears. We aren't just training to run; we are training to make our minds tougher. Pushing through the hard, ugly, imperfect stuff creates confidence and strength. It helps us understand and believe that just about anything is possible, if you work hard enough, fight long enough. That's why I love trail running. You don't have to be fast or elegant or naturally talented or have a ton of money or a particular body type. You just have to be tough, brave, and persistent. As we were checking in with Spencer, I realized I was starting to shake from having been so scared. Come within a couple of miles of the finish line, then, because something unexpected had happened, quit short of the goal and jump into a warm car?

HELL NO!

I did not want that narrative tagging along in my head for the future. I wanted to know I could keep on going, even though I was frightened and cold and exhausted. It was really important that I finish. All of that went through my head. I don't have a clue what I said out loud. I do recall that, as Erica and I started heading for the school, she simply said, "This is where your real training begins. Let's run to the school." We ran. We shuffled, hiked, and ran our way back to that finish area and straight to the nearest porta-potties (priorities). And then into the warm car.

We ran 32 miles in eight hours, 36 minutes. It was a beautiful, happy, memorable day of running. Day one of the Western States Training Camp was in the books. The three days of training camp as a whole were fantastic. Life-changing. I loved every minute of it. Okay, maybe not every single moment. There was that lightning, there was exhaustion, and there was a snake that made an unwelcome intrusion and caused both Erica and I to crash into the bushes. But less-than-fun moments are some of the best teachers. And some fantastic memories. I love those challenging times. They are the ones I draw upon, learn from, and use to help me become a better person, and a stronger runner over time. A person can learn a lot in their discomfort zone.

Chasing a Finish

"DNF." If you've ever run a race, you probably know what those three little letters mean, and are shaking your head in sympathy: Did Not Finish.

In July 2015, I tackled my first 50-mile run, the Siskiyou Out Back, better known as the S.O.B. And it is indeed a Son of a Bitch. I made it 41 miles and missed a course time cutoff. After ten hours and seventeen minutes, my race was over, and not by my choice.

Ultrarunning, as I've mentioned, is anything longer than a marathon (26.2 miles). By the time of the S.O.B., I had done several 50Ks (31 miles). Some other friends were hoping to crush the 100-mile distance in September. I have friends who have run 200-milers. The combinations, terrain, and distances are endless, mind-blowing really, in the world of ultrarunning. I was utterly in love with this sport, the people, and the community. But at that moment, in the Siskiyou Mountains, sitting on the side of the Pacific Crest Trail where it crossed over a forest road, I was trying to get my mind around a DNF. This was my first. And it wouldn't be my last. I heard a long-time ultrarunner say "You aren't an ultrarunner until you've had your first DNF.' Well then, call me an ultrarunner.

Mile 41. Here's the snapshot in my head as I crested the hill approaching the Siskiyou Gap aid station after running for ten hours. I see the tent in a small clearing, straddling the single-track. A woman who had been running just ahead of me for several miles is sitting on her knees, her head in her hands. Five experienced ultrarunner volunteer faces look up at me as I come out of the trees, and three start shaking their heads slightly. I didn't even really need to hear their words: "I'm sorry. Your day is done." This was my first DNF, ever. It really was an S.O.B. And it turns out that not meeting your goals can be one hell of a great teacher once you get over the shock and sadness of missing the goal. What did I learn? And how do I apply the lessons to my training and to my next race?

One of my top lessons came from a conversation with a seasoned ultrarunner, who was volunteering at the aid station where I DNF'd. He kindly sat with me for quite a while. He said he knew I wouldn't immediately understand what he was saying, but at some point, it would sink in. Here is what he told me: "You've trained hard. You've logged countless miles and hours, learned, and practiced. You've fallen more in love with the sport and with your body's ability to work hard. You've seen new trails, met new people, pushed boundaries, and gained strength. You showed up and toed the line when others were too scared to sign up. And you ran 41 miles today. No matter how today went, no one can take any of that away from you. It's yours. You earned it. Today is just one more day in the process of being an ultrarunner."

I don't think I have to tell anyone that it hurts the heart to miss a goal that one has worked hard for. I was crushed, embarrassed, frustrated. However, I was not defeated. That's a very important distinction. I would do this again. All my thinking was on scrambling to figure out where I screwed up, what I needed to improve upon, and how to fix it for the next ultra.

This race is where I made a new trail running friend and got damn good, sage advice that still rings in my ears on those days when training is hard. By early that evening, I was reminded that my friends and family of runners are pretty spectacular. The race turned out to be a fantastic training run on stunning trails, and another character-building experience in this whole process of embracing and living a healthy lifestyle. And no one can take any of that away from me.

Goodbye, Laziness

The Mac 50K is my favorite race, in one of my favorite places in the world: the McDonald-Dunn Forest, Corvallis Oregon. I approached it in 2016 as a long and supported practice run for the 100-mile event I had planned in September. I was testing gear, making sure of my shoe choice, practicing my newfound skills at running downhill, and working on fueling. This was my chance to put it all together and watch it work. It was fantastic. Cool, rainy, muddy. Friends, laughter. Perfection.

Running the Mac 50K in the McDonald-Dunn Forest.

In the back of my mind was the time I had run the event the previous year: eight hours and four minutes. Although I was trying to ignore that time — because this was a training run, not a race — it was an unstated goal for me to break eight hours.

Fueling was better than it had ever been. My gut stayed intact (I didn't shit my pants.). I loved my running shoes (and I still had all of my remaining toenails!). I was comfortable with my hydration pack, and I knew where to stash everything. I finally got to run an entire 50K with my friend and running partner, Josh. Wendie, his wife, paced both of us for the last five miles from The Saddle, the final aid station, after cheering and crewing for us all day. And Spencer, well, he placed eighth overall. He had a fantastic run. It was, like I said, a perfect day.

By the last leg of the race, everyone was muddy and tired. The finish line was looking really good. I had slipped and fallen in the mud at least three times — with laughter echoing through the woods as others were doing the same thing. Once I went down, stiff as board, flat on my face when my adductors cramped. Adductors are in the upper, inner thighs. And when they cramp, you literally get semi-paralyzed legs, with no warning. Josh, standing over me, laughing in sympathy, helpfully tells me as I lay on the ground writhing in pain, "Bets, damn it. Tell me next time you're going to do this so I can get my phone out and take a picture." So helpful. I think I might have tried to kick at him with my good leg in that moment and went back to writhing around in the mud trying to get the cramps to stop. With the cramp and the other slips-n'-falls, I was unhurt, but I was a total ball of mud, head to toe.

Josh knew I didn't want to talk about breaking eight hours, even though I could see him assessing the situation. We were appropriately tired, but totally healthy. We could pull it off if we picked up the pace. I was still trying to ignore it. A portion of my brain was totally fine with not achieving that goal. If we were to rise to the challenge, we would have to run consistently and fairly hard for the remainder of the course. That would mean a lot of work at the end of a day of hard work. I didn't have to cross the finish line to consider the day a smashing success. It had been huge already. And as I was starting to push the edges, with Josh speeding up, my brain was busy trying to convince me that we didn't need to put in any extra effort. "Just walk, Bets," my brain was saying. "You're going to finish close to last year's time, anyway. Close is good. Just being out here is enough."

I recognized those subtly negative voices in my head. I knew they were trying to shut things down. Brain management is very much a part of training for ultras. It takes practice to keep your head from talking you out of completing what you've set out to do with running an ultra. This is always both scary and fascinating. Sometimes, my brain drags out the big guns and I really have to fight just to keep breathing and moving. This time—in a race that was a practice run, one in which I was surrounded by friends I trusted deeply—I decided to just watch and see what demon trick my head was going to try to drag into the light. I had done a few races by now. I could say that I had been here before, in some form or fashion. I knew that at this point, I simply had to buckle down and keep moving forward as best I could. And I have learned numerous tricks to help me ignore or quiet the chatter in my head when it isn't productive or healthy or nice. I usually just try to blank out without fully defining whatever weapon my brain has chosen. I count steps, breathe, and try my best to ignore the tricks my head is playing.

This time my brain went straight to my old friend, laziness: "Take it easy. You've earned easy. There's no harm in just walking at this point." And I recognized laziness instantly. It was pretty cool to define it, understand it, then just accept it for what it is. I have had years of practice being lazy. It's my natural go-to. At this point in the race, 26- plus miles in, my legs and back were screaming for me to just ... stop ... running. My belly wasn't thrilled. My feet hurt. I had these obnoxious and painful adductor cramps violently grabbing hold of my upper inner thigh and stopping me dead in my tracks a few times. I didn't bother trying to evict or ignore the thoughts. I sure as hell didn't give in. I just decided to run with it.

When I'm on a training run (and my coach has given me parameters), I always go straight for the middle or "easy" end of whatever it is that I've been told to work on. Run ten or 12 minutes at race pace means I would aim to run 11:59 and call it good. Unless specifically told to do so, I rarely push to the upper limits or beyond. It's a subtle, persistent form of laziness. Training to run ultras is hard work in itself. I've struggled to get to this point, lose weight, and reverse diabetes. Does it really matter if I'm just a tad bit lazy about some aspects of training?

Josh would have none of that. He pushed me to give my all in the last five miles. At one point, I remember him turning around and just catching my eye and nodding his head roughly toward the finish line — about five miles away. We'd run together enough at this point that I knew this meant "Going for it — stay on my heels." I ran a freaking great run. All this effort going on in my head, battling and understanding laziness, was fantastic and constructive. I kept right on the heels of Josh, pushing hard to the finish. I put down faster miles at the end than I had most of the day. And I broke the eight-hour barrier.

As I ran, I had this idea clanging around in the back of my head: I am so freaking capable of being and doing so much more. If I'm given the chance to push hard, do I always give it my all? Or do I sometimes get lazy? It's an idea that I just can't let go of. What exactly would I be capable of, if I refused to let laziness win?

After I got home, Spencer and I were debriefing the race. I walked through the pieces that went great: fuel, shoes, handling the wicked leg cramps, ignoring the negative talk in my head, and pushing hard at the end of the race. I was able to manage the slides and the muddy, steep terrain. And then I ran faster miles at the end. I was really proud of my effort. I told Spencer that I acknowledge my tendency to get lazy in some of the targeted runs during a training cycle. I cheat myself and aim for "just good enough," simply by following the basic instructions instead of really testing my limits. I was going to work on learning to push myself harder when given the choice. I confessed that I know I sometimes let myself off the hook, when I really should be capitalizing on the opportunity to push to another level; it's a good thing to practice and get more comfortable with for a bunch of reasons. I've come so far, and I'm more in love with trail running than ever. My body is doing things I never, ever thought she was capable of. I know without a doubt that I am capable of still more strength and growth and change. Laziness isn't going to win this race.

Team Gum. One of many treasured race pictures and adventures.

Rocky Mountain High

August 3, 2016.

I am piling up clothing, shoes, and supplies because I am about to pack a bag and embark on an adventure (okay, so I use the singular phrase "a bag" euphemistically. Packing light is not one of my talents.). This is an epic adventure that I've been working toward for two years. It's cheesy to say, but it's kind of a dream-come-true moment for me. I leave in a matter of hours. My heart beats a little faster when I get asked about it. I break out in a big-ass grin. I've been walking around randomly humming "Rocky Mountain High" (I know it's not just about the mountains ... but I am a girl who grew up listening to John Denver on vinyl.).

Over the years, I have flown a ton for work. I have worked mostly west of the Mississippi River, flying in and out of Portland, Oregon. Oftentimes, I connected through a flight hub in Denver. Coming in and out of that airport, we would soar over the Colorado Rockies. There were many, many times that I stared out the window at those incredible mountains, thinking "I wonder what it would be like to actually be IN those mountains? How would it feel to climb up one of those exposed ridges, and feel as though I could turn 360 degrees and see the ends of the earth?"

With my weight at close to 400 pounds, looking out the window felt like the closest I would ever get to those fabled peaks. I'd never even dared to dream I might one day run in those mountains. Life has a way of changing. I no longer weigh 400 pounds. I'm not diabetic, dragging along a sharps container and pen needles. I don't even get winded and red-faced after walking half a mile. I'm active and healthy and ... I want to see those mountains! I want to know those mountains. I want to walk among them, breathe in that (thin!) air, and just see what it looks like from the ground ... not from the plexiglass window of an airplane.

So, I am going to Colorado for a running event. I'm headed to the TransRockies Run, a six-day stage race in the heart of the Rockies. I am traveling with my Oregon running friends Spencer, Dave, Erica, and Sean. For six days, we get to run, camp, make new friends, and immerse ourselves in the mountains. We will see, learn, and run 120 miles of those mountains. That will involve about 20,000 vertical feet of climbing in, on and around the Rockies. This is all one big happy adventure with another purpose; I am also gearing up for my first 100-miler in September. I am going to use this as one hell of a training block to be ready for that race. Win, win, win.

Dave, Erica, Sean, me, Spencer. TransRockies 2016.

It's epic. It's scary. It's exciting. I've never done anything like this in my life. I never thought I could do something like this in my life. But now I can! And you have absolutely no idea how badly I want to. Funny how your "fat" brain talks you out of things as impossible and improbable, and when you get healthy suddenly the blinders come off and you start thinking impossible and improbable sound like fun.

In my old life, I wouldn't have been in shape to hike anything beyond the parking lot. I couldn't sit in a car for 120 miles without being in extreme discomfort. I couldn't fit in a sleeping bag. Had I tried to sleep on the ground on a sleeping pad, I might never have gotten back up. I would not have trusted the camp to feed me enough sugar, fat, and processed foods. I never would have fit in a portable shower stall.

But that's no longer my reality. I'm really going to try to absorb each moment. I intend to enjoy every single step I take in those fabled, rugged, and spectacular mountains. I have worked steadily for two years to get to the point where I can run the mileage and handle the back-to-back-to-back days of running. I know I fit in my sleeping bag, and I'm looking forward to the healthy food that will be served. Now, it's time to meet those mountains with my very own feet.

"The mountains are calling, and I must go." — John Muir

Rediscovering Joy in the Rockies

For weeks after TransRockies, I thought about the incredible experience, missing my new friends, and wishing I could live in a tent and run all day, every day. I told Kevin "Houda" McDonald, the race director, that his epic "adult running camp" had ruined reality for me.

I found myself. Found deep joy on trails I had only ever seen from an airplane window. I even found a yeti, a cheerleading yeti, named Fitzy. I reveled in each and every step of each and every run. I worked for more than two years to get to the point that I could endure and enjoy six straight days of running and camping. In a tent, surrounded by other trail runners from across the globe. At Camp Hale, Colorado, I was in heaven.

But if you backtrack a few weeks before TransRockies. I had a training week from hell, by design. I had to do a "big volume" week, nearly a 100 miles, which I had never done before. I allowed the fatigue and negative energy from that week of hard physical and mental work to cascade down. I had a full-on meltdown the end of that week and told Spencer I never wanted to run again. I also said things like I wanted to sell all my shoes, never wear a running shirt again, and that I was unfriending anyone who posted about running on Facebook. It was pretty epic. Totally ridiculous now, of course, but in that moment, I actually felt it! It was joyless, exhausting, and scary as hell. I felt apathetic. And apathy scares me more than anything.

Back to the Rockies, as I was running on day one of this epic six-day adventure, I began acknowledging that I had slowly snuffed out my own joy in running. And when I figured it out I willingly ditched that grumpy, nasty piece of work in a creek. The creek was cold and swift and beautiful and the ideal place to let that ugliness quickly and quietly wash away without contaminating anyone else in the process. I suddenly felt free and light and happy. I had found my joy again! I missed her. I missed her so very much! My mind was suddenly excited to see what the trails would be like, who I would meet, and what I would learn. There were no time requirements for any of the stages and no real plan for each day, other than to give my best and practice what I'd spent the past few years learning. I met great people. I took a ton of pictures. I soaked it all in. And I ran straight toward the joy I used to have in my early days of running. Joy welcomed me back like a grateful, forgiving, and long-lost friend.

The night we arrived at TransRockies, Spencer gave me his coaching brief. Usually, a pre-race briefing goes something like this: "Do not stop and pick up rocks. No selfies. Don't waste time in aid stations. Limit conversations. If you can talk while you run or hike, you aren't working hard enough. Eat often and plenty. Stick to the plan." This time, he looked me squarely in the eye and said, "Bets, I want you to just breathe, listen, and do not respond to what I'm going to say. This week is going to change your life if you let it. Get to know everyone you meet, pick up heart-shaped rocks, take pictures, stop and thank all the volunteers, and just enjoy each and every step of the journey."

I listened. With my whole heart, I listened.

Each stage felt life-changing and healing, like a reunion of the happiest kind. Stage five, as you know, is where I found myself and ditched the former 400-pound woman on the ridge above Vail. That was when I finally knew, beyond any shadow of a doubt, that I was a trail runner.

That week changed me. I let it.

Me, Michelle and Andie. TransRockies.

7 CHAPTER SEVEN
100 MILES

"Write a note to yourself while you are so excited. In those rare, fleeting, or dark moments when you aren't excited, when you're exhausted or feel scared or unsure, you can look back and read your very own words and remember this moment. Remember the why."

This was the sage advice of my mentor and friend, Peg Herring. She also said, "I do not understand what you have chosen to do. Not at all. But you need to know that I support you 100 percent. You can do anything you set out to do." Here's the note I wrote myself:

Bets,

You just, like 20 minutes ago, signed up for the Mountain Lakes 100-mile race. Now you get to spend the next eight months training! Then, on September 24, 2016, you get to freaking toe the line! You are wholeheartedly, bone-deep excited. Giddy, even. You spent the week walking around, grinning ear-to-ear. You have gone to bed each night happy and very much at peace with your decision to embark on this wild adventure.

Josh Gum planted the idea in your head to run a 100-miler about three years ago. He introduced you to the idea of ultras and endurance sports. "You don't have to go fast," he said. "You just can't give up." The idea that you might be able to run 100 miles – you, Bets, the once morbidly obese girl, the diabetic who swore she hated running – this idea has become an obsession and a deep-seated desire. Since the day the seed was planted, you've been wondering, dreaming, becoming focused on the idea that maybe, just maybe, you might have it in your heart and soul (and legs) to actually run something obnoxiously, audaciously, fantastically long, like a 100-miler.

For the last three years, you have been dedicated to learning the art and sport of running. And while you're just barely getting started, that hasn't stopped you from totally falling in love with trail running in the process. Falling in love with all of it. The people, the sport, the experiences, the miles, the challenge. Every single thing about trail running appeals to you, speaks to you, heals and nourishes and strengthens your soul.

You have also learned that this life adventure is not just about running. This whole process of getting ready for, and tackling, a 100-miler is really about wondering if you have the fortitude and ability to take a really big, scary goal and tackle it, own it, beat it. This is about putting your hard-fought lifestyle changes to the test. It's about getting stronger, brain and body. It is about really LIVING your life.

You spent your 20s, 30s, and into your early 40s as a morbidly obese, 399-pound diabetic. You were always saying to yourself, "I can't run." "I can't do that." "I am too fat to do that." "I am pretty sure that would hurt." "I am too old." Here's the kicker: how can you really hate, or deny, or be fearful of something you have never done? Be honest with yourself, Bets. You had never gone running. You weren't eating healthy. You weren't being active. You weren't doing anything long enough to form an actual, honest-to-goodness opinion of your own. You were just accepting the passive opinions about your abilities and limitations based upon ASS-umptions. Well, you're done assuming. This effort will require that you give your very best on every single possible level. It will test everything you think you are made of. People you love, trust, and respect have told you, warned you, not-so-gently reminded you that this is going to test things you never knew were going to be tested, that you never dreamed you would encounter. This will change you.

Remember what Josh said? "It's going to be an experience that will change you in ways that will surprise you." You are ready for that testing. Not just on race day, because you will be tested every step of the way during the training process, too. Gaining new distances, building your core and back, learning to fuel, endless practice running down hills, even more endless practice with speed work, running uphill, power hiking.

You want to hit that start line for the Mountain Lakes 100 knowing that you kept putting in your best effort every single time you put on your running shoes. If you commit 100 percent to the training, you can put all of that together on race day, and enjoy the magic that happens when hard work and a heartfelt goal start racing in the same direction.

You did not just sign up for this on a whim. You have been tenaciously, intentionally and consistently working up to a fitness level where you feel wholeheartedly ready to train for, and do, your first 100-miler. You spoke with Spencer at length about what you wanted to do, more than two years ago.

With guidance from both Spencer and Josh, you decided you had the perfect race in your sights when you picked Mountain Lakes for your first 100-miler. You know you can do this. Spencer says you're ready to train to run the 100-miler. Team Gum (Josh and Wendie) have said they know you are up to the task and will support you 100 percent. That's all the external validation you wanted or needed to eagerly hit the "Sign me up now!" button. Now, go throw your heart and feet onto the trails, and get training for this sucker.

When times get dark or scary or daunting, you will look back on this note and remember what you were thinking and feeling.

This is not just about running. It has never, ever been entirely about running. This whole amazing adventure is about something much, much bigger. It's about owning and chasing down a dream. It's about believing in yourself. It's about intentionally choosing to push into new, scary territory. It's about living life to the fullest, each and every day.

Mountain Lakes

This was it: the race I had been aiming at for years. This distance of a race was in my brain almost since I began running, and this specific race was in my brain for over a year. I chose Mountain Lakes 100 because Spencer and Josh both thought it was a great choice for a first attempt at the 100 mile distance. Beginning at the Olallie Lake Resort in the Oregon Cascades, with much of the track on the Pacific Crest Trail, it was a local race for me. It had great race directors with Todd and Renee Janssen of Go Beyond Racing, and was at a time of year when Spencer, Josh, and Wendie could all help me. I had plenty of time to train. Local running friends had experience with the race and terrain. The biggest training block I would need to make it happen was already built in, with the summer's TransRockies event. It was perfect.

I signed up. All the stars aligned. 100-milers were totally new, unknown and scary as hell! I had a few goals going into this race:

- Finish before the 30-hour cutoff.

- As my trail-running friend and accomplished ultrarunner Ken Ward suggested, start slow, don't slow down. Finish strong.

- Get to my crew in pre-designated windows of time.

- Get to and from aid stations efficiently, and do not waste time.

- Stay happy and smiling, and maintain a good attitude. This is the most important to me. I sometimes get sharp and snarky when I get scared or embarrassed. I wanted to be the happy runner from mile 0 to 100, even if this was the scariest thing I had ever done.

- Stay on track with my carefully calculated fueling plan: energy gels every 20 minutes (for 30 hours, that means 90 gel packets.).

- Eat solid fuel at aid stations and with crew.

- Drink plenty of water.

- When I hike, it will be strong, with purpose and intention.

- Run the downhills.

- Enjoy the experience. This has been one hell of a journey. The race is about that journey, not about a destination.

Here's my race report.

Mile 0 to 5.3. The weather is beautiful, and off I go! It's 8 a.m. on Saturday. The run begins over a rutted forest road. I am running the same pace as Roger, a Corvallis runner. We chat about our strategies, our excitement, and the wisdom that others have passed on to us. I focus on walking up any hills. We wish each other luck. I would spend the rest of the day trying to chase Roger down. We turn onto single track. We climb over downed trees and across narrow rock ledges. I'm told it was a beautiful section. I am carefully watching my feet.

Mile 5.3 to 11.4. I quickly check in and out of Aid Station One. It is followed by a downhill section of forest road — shady, smooth, and so runnable! Experienced runners have told me that, if at any point in the first 50 miles of a 100-miler, you question whether you're pushing too hard, then you are. Back off. I try to stay aware of this as I run comfortably downhill, chill and easy. I chat with some great folks around me. We're all pretty fresh and hyped to be doing this.

Mile 11.4 to 20.75. I make my first mistake at Aid Station Two. I think I have enough water for the long climb ahead (nine miles, 2,600-foot ascent). Instead of refilling, I choose to get ahead of a pack of people onto the single track. Around mile 18, I discover that I am out of water. In the increasing heat, my fuel choice doesn't do well without water. I puke up one energy gel then skip one. I go for almost an hour without fuel or water. Dumb. I pull out my trekking poles to help me work the uphill. I hike with intention and stay focused on getting the first 25 miles done well, to set a good tone for the rest of the race. I feel as though I am settling into, and enjoying, the task at hand. I get to spend some time on the trail with my good friend Rita. And on this stretch of trail I meet, and be deeply encouraged by, the incredible Terry Abrams, a six-times Badwater-135 Finisher, eternal optimist, and tough-as-nails runner.

Mile 20.75 to 26.05. I run back to Olallie Lake, the start and the finish line staging area, on the familiar roads we had run out on from the start. My fuel is staying down, I have water again, and I'm super excited to be headed back to my crew! This is the first time since I started that I will see them. Weeks of tension about getting to the start line have evaporated, and I am simply overjoyed at the thought of seeing Spencer, Josh, and Wendie. Suddenly I hear Wendie's familiar "Whoop! Whoop!" She runs up to me with flat Coke in a polka-dot cup. I could kiss her. She leads me through the aid station to our crew car. Spencer runs up to see what else I need. I should be calm and thoughtful, but I am spastic and erratic; my friends are here!!! They stay focused and get me refueled, watered, and stocked up. We deal with some potentially annoying chafing in the hind-end area, then I am back on the trail. Of the entire race, the thrill of seeing those faces I love so dearly—starting nerves gone, a smart race underway—remains one of my most favorite snapshot memories.

Mile 26.05 to 29.15. There's a thing in ultrarunning called "bonus miles." You don't want bonus miles. You collect them when you go off-course or get lost. I pick up about half a bonus mile when I leave my crew and simply miss the turn for the next segment. A car is parked directly in front of the trailhead for the perfectly marked Pacific Crest Trail (PCT). I'll be forever grateful to the angel (the wife of a trail runner who was in the race with me) who got out of her nearby car, chased me down in her flip-flops, and got me turned around. I have to work to not let that little detour shake my confidence. Back on course, I start running the exposed ridges of the PCT, realizing I will see my crew again shortly ... and then not for hours. Josh told me to spend the run segment organizing my thoughts about what I need for nightfall. I do just that.

Mile 29.15 to 36.65. At the next aid station, I change shirts and make sure I have pants stuffed into my pack because I'll be running into the dark hours before I see my crew again. That's a big deal for me, publicly stripping down to a sports bra in front of strangers at the aid station. But the front of my shirt is wet from a faulty/leaky water nib on my hydration vest, and I'm headed into what's going to be a dark, cool run. With fuel replenished, headlamp in the pack, dry shirt and pants in the pack, I am off again. These next miles are imminently runnable and enjoyable. I feel comfortable and smart about how I plan to tackle the terrain in front of me with what daylight I have left.

Mile 36.65 to 43.85. I grab some solid food at the next aid station, fill up my hydro vest, and scramble out fast. I can't believe how easily I'm moving, well past the 50K mark. I am starting to feel some pain and fatigue, especially in my feet which are beginning to feel every rock on the path; but all things considered, I feel pretty darn good. I am getting miles put down while the sun is still up, and I can see the trail. Things will naturally slow once I'm using a headlamp.

Miles 43.85 to 49.35. As evening falls, I put my headlamp on. Before long, I kick a rock and go down to my knees, trying to catch my breath. This isn't depressing or defeating, but the pain in my feet and my increased caution slow me down more than I'd like. I get aggressive with my trekking poles and let them do some work. In a way, I run this section using my arms, bearing weight on the poles to get a little hop over the rough terrain and give my feet an additional one-second rest with each assisted hop. I find it entertaining and distracting. The elite, lead runners, having made the turn at mile 60-plus, are now charging back down the out-and-back section of the trail to the finish line. In the dark, their oncoming torches are beautiful and deeply comforting. You know you're headed in the right direction when returning runners come toward you. At the next aid station, my friend Jason Leman, an elite ultrarunner, kind-hearted soul, and die-hard volunteer is wearing a gold lamé Elvis onesie. He is a sight for sore eyes. Since he is an experienced runner, I tell him I'm fighting nausea. He encourages me to drink some ginger ale and eat solid food before leaving the station. I do all of that and almost instantly feel better. He gives me a huge hug and tells me to keep cranking.

Miles 49.35 to 54.65. Now I am totally in the dark, moving as fast as I can while descending a technical section of trail. From the next aid station, Wendie will be pacing me through a 16-mile loop around Timothy Lake. Meanwhile, heading for the crew and the lake, I start to wonder how I'm doing with time: have I slowed down too much? One's mind plays tricks in the dark. You hear things, you worry you're lost, that you've lost track of time. You wonder why you're doing this crazy thing at all. I am just starting to wonder how the rest of this adventure will play out, if I am behind the pace with my feet getting increasingly sore. Instead of recalling the plan I created, and forcing those ideas into my head, I begin to buy into a different story — that this adventure is actually being written as I run, and that I have control only over my own forward motion and how I choose to react to whatever might happen.

Miles 54.65 to 60.65. As I near the aid station at Clackamas Ranger Station around 11 p.m., I hear Spencer yelling for me out of the darkness. Hearing his voice, after fifteen hours of running, is one of the best sounds in the world. Spence asks what I need, and I ask him if we can take off my shoe and look at my foot. The toe looks sore but normal, he says. I may have imagined him saying, "Suck it up, Buttercup!" I ask for ibuprofen and solid food. Spencer says my time is right on target. He crams food into my hands and tells me to get a move on. Wendie, my pacer (whom I've been waiting all day to see!), takes off with me. With her by my side, time and miles fly by. She's my soul/sole sister and we laugh and chat and simply enjoy each other's company at midnight, running around a lake in the middle of the Cascades. With me in the lead, we arrive at a series of bridges going over creeks leading into the lake. I step off the edge of one and yelp, "Steep drop off!" She follows me carefully. When we turn back to look, we see that the drop is only about seven inches. While it may have been funny, I know I am fatigued and it is only going to get worse.

Miles 60.65 to 66.25. We are in and out of the next aid station at Little Crater Lake in about 90 seconds. Wendie runs ahead and takes charge of pointing out what she thinks I need. It is perfect teamwork. We're trying really hard not to waste time as we follow sweet, groomed single track around Timothy Lake, just south of Mt. Hood, to a dam where Spencer and Josh will be waiting at the next aid station. Wendie sings (badly). I am chewing Big Red gum after violently gagging on an orange energy gel. Wendie coaxes me gently, and then not so gently, to keep moving at a decent clip: "The boys are waiting for us," she says. "Let's surprise them and get there early." If I were more experienced, or perhaps in better shape, or if it was daylight, I would find this section really runnable. Although I'm hiking as fast as I can and jogging in stretches, I can't string together any runs of decent length. My feet are sore; I start to feel as if my legs need to be told to work, and I am taking a lot of brain power to keep them moving.

Miles 66.25 to 70.95. Two sights greet us as we arrive at the wildly lit-up aid station at Timothy Lake Dam—two great, white full moons. One provided by the universe. One was Josh. A sight I may never be able to clear from my brain. He leads us to the car where Spencer has everything set. It's now 1 a.m. or so on Sunday morning. Wendie helps me pull on my running pants, as it is now cold and I don't want to take my shoes off. In the dark, everyone is wearing their headlamps. We hear music from the aid station behind us. Spence force-feeds me Top Ramen from a Hydro Flask. As Josh gets her ready for the next leg, Wendie tries to repair my dead torch. All my favorite people are taking care of one another, to get just one of us (me!) to her goal. That image provides a silent, powerful emotion that I reflect upon many, many times in the coming hours. Josh will take over the pacing from Wendie at the next aid station. Wendie and I take off. Things get tough when I hit my first "low" soon after leaving the dam. I quietly begin to question myself, whether I can leg out another 30-plus miles with an ascent of more than 3,000 feet ahead, and do it before a cutoff. I know I've run smart and hard to this point, and I have done everything as right as I possibly can. There is a sense of heaviness and fear. Ahead is what this beast is really all about. I worry I may not be entirely up to the task. But I want this so, so badly … Wendie reminds me to breathe, asks what hurts, offers gum and reminds me to eat food. Finally, she just asks: "Are you okay being quiet with your pain, B?" I say yes. I don't know how to tell her I can handle the physical pain, that it's my head I am battling. I'm afraid that putting it into words will make it real. So I stay quiet, grappling to find a positive foothold to climb out of this particular low spot.

As we approach the next station, Spencer runs out to greet me and see what I need for the next segment; Wendie goes ahead, alerting Josh to get ready to run. I tell Spencer about my "low." He says it's okay; lows happen. You've trained for this. You knew this would happen. Keep moving forward, keep breathing through it, he says. He reminds me of how badly I want the finish line. With all my heart, I want that finish line. I tell him that. I know this low is simply a new set of emotions setting in to keep me company for the rest of the run. I tell Spencer my mantra now is: "Shut up brain! Get the hell out of the way and let your legs run!" I will tell myself that, over and over and over, for the next ten hours.

Miles 70.95 to 76.25. I arrive at the aid station at the Clackamas Ranger Station fifteen minutes ahead of schedule, about fifteen minutes ahead of the official cutoff. So it's really important that I make this stop quick and keep moving. I hug Wen goodbye and grab some food. Then Josh and I waste no time in hitting the trails again. Josh will stay with me for the next 30 miles until I cross the finish line. A mile or two in, we begin a long, slow climb in the dark. I find myself losing speed with each step. Instead of using my trekking poles, I am dragging them. Josh begins to run through paces and times. He's telling me, gently and kindly, that we have to move faster if I am going to make the finish line. In the dark, anxiety and panic smash into my chest. I begin to cry — quietly, for miles. Josh gently reminds me to use my trekking poles on the uphill. For the next 30 miles, he continually reminds me to use my trekking poles, to keep moving and to eat and drink. He has his hands full, and we have at least nine more hours to go. I begin to feel very guilty. When I asked Josh, my first trail-running friend, to pace me on this adventure, I had no idea what kind of runner I would be, how much work I would be asking him to do. The PCT, running back toward Olallie Lake, should be familiar. In the dark, it doesn't feel that way. My brain is relieved to have someone else in charge. I have abdicated responsibility for myself into the hands of someone I trust with my life. I am using all my energy to fight the mental fog and fear in my brain, and to just stay present.

Miles 76.25 to 81.75. As first morning light begins to glow pink on the horizon, we encounter the next aid station on a long, sustained climb. I am beginning to obsess about times, paces, and miles. I grab a Fig Newton and briefly flop into a chair when my friend Jason reappears. He hugs me, reminds me I can now turn off my torch, and helps me figure out where to stow it in my pack. Then he lies to me, telling me how great I look, how strong I am, how well I am doing. I will forever love him for that exchange. Josh tells me time is up. I force myself up and out of the chair and we leave. I want to stay. I want to cry. What would happen if I just stop running here? Would my friends still love me? I realize, though, that this is not helpful or useful thinking. I know I must stop thinking about quitting, and focus instead on how to keep pain from commandeering my thoughts. I need to concentrate on that finish line.

Miles 81.75 to 88.95. Then I hit a major low that doesn't let me go until just before the finish line. I fight every step. I cry. I sob. I keep moving. At one point, Josh asks, "How's your heart? How badly do you really want this B?" He lets me stew. He changes topics. He reminds me to eat. He coaxes me to run. He is never more than about five feet away, even when I have to step off the trail to pee. The sun has risen and the temperature is warming. As I run, every step is jarring. I begin to involuntarily whimper and groan with every step. I can't stop it, and it's annoying me. "Just let it happen!" says Josh. "This is painful and tough, and there's no judgment if it propels you on." I'm confused that I have no control over it. As we near the next aid station, Josh reminds me that we really don't need anything and we should keep moving. He isn't panicked about time, but he is watching it, adjusting for the fact that I am slowing down in each segment.

Miles 88.95 to 96.45. After a series of rolling ups and downs, I am getting warm and the morning warms up. I am thirsty and running out of water. It seems I can't get enough to drink. Josh is reminding me to eat. Every once in a while, one of the chews falls out of my mouth as I try to eat or breathe. Josh accuses me of spitting them out; I was not! We laugh. We pass a volunteer who says it's 4.4 miles to the next aid station. She fails to mention it's almost all uphill. I am whiny and totally annoyed with myself.

Another runner, Daisy Clark, runs past. We realize we've only ever known each other on social media and are thrilled to be meeting in person! She taps me lightly on the back, makes eye contact with me and in a quiet and fierce voice she tells me, "You have this. Do not stop." Another trail-sister friendship of a lifetime is born in that moment. A few times, I earnestly try to run. All I can manage are three or four steps of running at a time. "Great job," Josh says. A few beats later, he says, "Let's try that again." When we hit the 90-mile mark, Josh says: "You're ten miles out! You're doing this! Can you believe it?" We settle into a pattern of me groaning or asking time, and Josh asking me to eat or run. It is companionable. I don't drop any F-bombs in his direction—a major victory as I have been known to cuss him out from time to time on a hard run. My goal to keep a good attitude from start to finish and with everyone I encountered in intact. The climb, it seems, is endless. When it finally does end, it seems like another four miles to the turnoff leading to the penultimate aid station. We run in, I grab some Coke, and Josh helps me fill my pack. Then I move toward the finish line for all I am worth.

Miles 96.45 to 100.95. It's Sunday mid-morning. I wish I could say I'm smiling and happy and calm, that I'm running the last 5K to the finish line. That would be a great ending to this adventure. It's not what happened. I believe this 4½-mile segment took about 90 minutes. Despite hot, exposed climbs and my pain and self-doubt, I keep moving forward, running as best I can, given the hours of wear on my legs and my obnoxiously sore feet. Seemingly out of nowhere, Spencer shows up to run in with us. I am so very happy to see him, but I don't know that I convey any of that.

I have a singular focus on ignoring the pain and moving forward, no matter what. Time seems to stretch out. I move slower, and even with intense coaxing, I can't seem to move any faster. People cheer us on as they pass. The trail will not end. At one point, Josh finally says, "You can hike this in, and we're still going to make it. Can you believe you're going to finish?" Again, the stupid, uncontrollable sobbing. No, I don't believe it. Not at all. At one point, I hunch over and just stop on the trail. Josh grabs my pack, gently pushes me forward and says something along the lines of, "Oh, no, you're not." "C'mon, Bets," says Spencer. "Keep moving. You've got this." I have a team of incredible power at my back, a team like no other. A team that loves me even when I am at my lowest possible point. They want me to get to the finish line as much as I myself want it. And I will do anything to keep from disappointing them. My mind is done. I am using all my energy just to get my legs to lift and move, lift, and move. Breathe. Repeat.

When we turn the final bend, I hear Wendie screaming for us! A quarter-mile from the finish, with about 25 minutes to spare before cutoff, I have no response to seeing this amazing woman and friend, other than to utter a quiet, somber, "Thank you." I cannot wrap my head around the fact that I might actually see the finish line after two days of running. As we break out onto a short section of road, my whole crew is with me. "C'mon," says Spence. "Let's run this in." We can hear the finish line. Then we can see the finish line. Then I finally turn to Josh and say, yes, I do believe I'm going to finish. And everyone gives a small, relieved laugh.

My friends, my support umbrella, join me as we run into a human-made finisher's chute. I cross the line in 29:40:19. I have just attempted and completed my very first 100-miler ... with 19 minutes and 41 seconds to spare.

Spencer, Wendie, me, Josh. 2016 Mountain Lakes 100.

8 CHAPTER EIGHT
ECHOES OF THE PAST

I recently pulled out my glucose-testing kit. It had been in retirement for three years. It was a bit of a low moment. I was sad and a little scared. I had a sudden flash of fear that diabetes was back, or trying really hard to creep back in. I had noticed some things that seemed disconnected, but hauntingly familiar. Fuzzy thinking. Thirsty. Sleepy. Insatiably hungry. Irritable, out-of-the-blue or out-of-proportion emotions. Craving sugar. Feeling "puffy." The symptoms seemed out of left field, given how careful I was being. I hadn't felt these symptoms in these odd clusters in more than three years. All of a sudden, it dawned on me why these were familiar: this is the crap that happened when my blood sugars were out of whack. Holy crap! It was time to test and see what the numbers had to tell me. I tested as soon as I put the pieces together. My post-prandial (two hours post-meal) glucose measured 111. For me, that's a solid number, if a tad bit high. It's respectable.

Whew. A little breathing room and a stab of relief.

I tested a fasting number the next morning, and it was 110. On the high side, but arguably good. I exhaled in relief. The next day, fasting was 100. I was in a "safe space" with the numbers I was seeing and recording. They were not as low as I would like, nor were they as low as I can make them when I'm keeping my diet "tight." While I was clinically in a non-diabetic range, I still felt pretty clearly that this was a wake-up call.

After the Mountain Lakes 100 in September 2016, I had a revelation of sorts. The conversation in my head — and out loud to Spencer — went sort of like this: "I just ran for a 100 miles, for close to 30 hours, and fueled that effort with about 5,000 to 6,000 calories of sugar. And while that's pretty typical running fuel for "normal" folks, I'm not metabolically normal. Not by a long shot. Holy shit! This is utterly asinine. It's a deadly circle. It's a recipe for disaster."

So I made the decision that I needed to change some things. Immediately. Back to basics. It all had to start with my day-to-day food plan. There's a health condition called "insulin resistance." It is also called "carbohydrate intolerance." I've done a ton of research on it, and I have come to understand that while I am no longer diabetic, I am still insulin resistant and always will be. I can certainly manage it, but it's not going to go away. While this is not an entirely accurate description, I kind of think of it as being allergic to carbs. I have to be very careful with my day-to-day diet. As well as careful with what I choose to use for fueling during races or adventures.

Now, here's the disclaimer. I'm an experiment of one. I lost more than 200 pounds, reversed type 2 diabetes, and somehow fell head over heels in love with the endurance running world. It turns out there aren't many people like me out there, and the "normal" rules for food, nutrition, and fueling just don't ever seem to work well for me. My solutions and chosen paths are not likely to work or make sense for anyone else. I'm well aware that I can't eat too much of any kind of carbs, even the healthy ones, no matter what anyone else says. You might think these are good for everyone and I'm overreacting to fruits or starchy veggies; my swinging blood sugars tell the truth. And I have to listen to my body. If I keep carbs to a minimum, my glucose stays in a horizontal and largely stable line.

So, goodbye to my plant-based diet that I loved and enjoyed for nearly three years, averaging 300 to 400 grams of carbs each day with a healthy balance of grains, fruits, and veggies. Hello again to my old friends, no-and-low carbs. I tightly restrict my daily carbohydrate load. I'm aiming for whole, non-processed foods as best I can; no-wrappers, few ingredients that should be totally recognizable and have a super short-shelf life. I am most especially vigilant for any of the added or hidden variations of sugars and corn syrups that were truly and absolutely my worst enemy as a type 2 diabetic.

I know how to do this. I just willingly and knowingly strayed from the basics that got me here. I strayed from the food plan that helped me lose weight, become non-diabetic, and learn to run. I suddenly felt free and healthy enough to try new things with food, fueling, and diet. I'm totally okay with those experiments and what they have taught me about myself and the way my body works. I find it humbling and interesting that I am back to where it all started, back to the very basics of what worked when I first started this journey. Back to low-carb, no-sugar, low-glycemic-index foods.

A Holiday Meltdown

Food owned me for 44 years. And the truth is, it still does at times. At the oddest, most random moments, a titanic wave of emotions about food may be triggered. I have been actively working on my relationship with food for many years. I want to have peace with food and eating. Right before the holidays in 2016, I had a meltdown. As it turned out, it was a productive, emotional meltdown that's ultimately moving me closer to that peaceful relationship with food that I'm pursuing. This one involved tears and about three days of emotional exhaustion as I sorted out what had happened. I learned something useful and positive about myself in the whole process. My coping mechanism this time around was conversation, with just a little bit of hiding and crying thrown in to keep things interesting. My coping mechanisms were not food or eating. That was a huge win.

So what happened to cause this meltdown?

I have always said I wasn't a secret eater — at least, not in the classic sense of making sure no one sees me physically eating and then hiding any evidence (such as burying trash, hiding candy wrappers, or dumping packaging at the grocery store). I would eat anything, unapologetically, in front of people. But I was my own version of a secret eater. For me, it was, "Don't let any single person have a clear picture of your eating habits." I've been very careful my whole adult life to make sure no individual knew my calorie count for the entire day. I was careful for decades. I'm a ninja at this crap. My thinking: if someone knew the totality of what I was eating, they would know with absolute certainty why I am fat. This was still my thinking.

Given my diabetes history, I'm still carb-phobic at times. Even though I am no longer diabetic, I still think about every bite of food in the form of counting calories and carbs. I still very much have a hard-wired list of foods that are labeled good or bad, that I chronically weigh every food choice against. Old habits die hard.

I tried my food-ninja routine with Spencer—who also happens to be my roommate as we work to get our business, Novo Veritas, off the ground and running. I was unconsciously careful to make sure that he didn't know the full picture of what I was eating each day. I didn't realize I was doing this at the time. Looking back, it was exactly what I was doing. And I was really good at it. Then Spencer caught me.

He did most of our grocery shopping at the time. We would prepare foods periodically to share, as we had the same eating habits and we were both eating a plant-based diet at the time. At my request, he was showing me some new foods to try for breakfast. I was sick of oatmeal. I remember I was being a bit squirmy. I needed help in finding some food options and variety. I was really working to lose some of my fears and rules around food, and Spencer was willing to help. But the desire to find food solutions was in a big-time battle with my not wanting Spencer (or anyone) to know what I was actually putting in my belly. Although I said I wanted help with breaking my self-imposed food rules and fears, I didn't honestly want that help. Spencer was totally unaware of my emotional baggage as he showed me how to build a good, plant-based, protein-packed breakfast bowl.

I was on my own for lunch, although Spencer had packed food in the fridge. Then dinner rolled around and the meltdown occurred. Spencer knew what I had eaten for breakfast and could easily figure out what I had for lunch. Now we were discussing what to eat for dinner. In the grand scheme of trying to hide my total calorie consumption for the day, I knew that Spencer could quickly calculate what I had just eaten for the entire day. Now, I do eat healthy foods. I'm focused on appropriately fueling my running and other activity. But my mind is not entirely healed, as you've probably figured out by now.

As I stood in the kitchen with Spencer, it dawned on me that my secretly screwed-up relationship with food was no longer safe and secure. That was a scary feeling. Spencer now knew what my calories were for the day. He knew the quality of the foods I ate. I quietly lost it. The tears I'd been fighting back all day were going to spill over. So I did what most healthy adult females would do. I went upstairs to my room, closed the door, and cried. I waited for a while, hoping he hadn't noticed anything amiss, and we could just go about business as usual. Not so much. He was waiting to talk to me.

"So, we've obviously uncovered some painful shit. You want to talk about it?"

Later, when I started therapy, I would identify this story as the singular moment I knew something was really wrong. This moment alarmed me because I knew deep down that something big was lurking. I would have to wade in and fight through an acute binge episode, and the exercise of "why I run" to begin to piece it all together, but this was the moment I remember cautiously admitting to myself there was something really, terribly broken. I was going to have to figure it out and stop ignoring it all. I sat down and choked on my dinner. I cried. I felt like I couldn't even begin to put into words how incredibly vulnerable I felt, not only because he knew what I had eaten for the day, but also because he wasn't going to just let me walk away without talking about it. Bastard. So we talked. Haltingly. Spencer patiently waited me out as I tried to find the words to explain what was happening. Tasting the words oh-so-carefully as I was spitting them out for the very first time. And I'm grateful that he gave me the gift of generous patience as I began to process 45 years of food issues out loud. He helped to safely and gently open the flood gates.

"The best way out is always through." – Robert Frost

Binge Eating

I still make myself laugh sometimes. I really thought, when I started this healthy lifestyle journey, that I would reach an "end," a finishing point. I thought some of the bad things would disappear and would no longer be an issue. The joke's on me. A weight on the scale? Behaviors that were banished or permanently changed? Some sort of finish line? I really had no idea what I thought the "end" would look like. I was so sure there would be one. I thought that once I got healthy, once I got to a normal weight, some of these problems would simply just disappear. They don't. Who knew?

An old friend came to visit in November 2017. "Old friend," of course, is a euphemism for "something shitty that I was really, fervently hoping I had forever eliminated from my life." I thought it was going to stay the hell away forever … and then it just knocked me on my ass. My old friend showed up again. I was, and I am, a binge eater. I had always dressed that up. When I had to say anything at all, I said I was a compulsive overeater. That is true; it's a component of the problem I battle. Overeating can be sporadic, with no guilt or shame attached to an overly full belly from time to time. It can just be a bad habit. Binge eating is an entirely different animal. According to *Healthline*, binge eating disorder (BED) is the most common eating disorder in the United States. It is a medical condition characterized by a loss of control over one's eating habits. People with BED regularly eat large amounts of food when they are not physically hungry, then feel guilty or ashamed after doing so. Hunger has nothing to do with it. Binge eating sucks. Big time.

For me, a binge gets started when I'm sad, when I'm not being active, when things in my life feel increasingly out of control. As that toxic combination takes command, I try to regain control through the comfort and "love" I find in food. Binge eating is a real issue, one we rarely discuss. I know from conversations, texts, emails, and Facebook messages that I don't suffer alone. A great many people are suffering quietly, and miserably, from binge eating.

I hadn't had a big binge since 2009, before my mom died. And I had never been formally diagnosed. I labeled it overeating, but hindsight proves these were classic binges. I had done some overeating in the intervening time, to be sure, but not a purposeful, yet uncontrollable, binge. I thought I had cured myself of binge eating, or at least buried it deep enough to be done with it. I thought it was totally under control. I was wrong.

Last year's binge caught me totally by surprise, though in retrospect there were plenty of warning signs. None of my new, healthy, hard-fought habits could stop it. It lasted four days, and it scared the shit out of me. No one knew I was bingeing. When I finally broke down and realized I needed help, I reached out to Spencer. He said, "I didn't know you were bingeing!" I replied, "That's because I didn't want you to know … I'm good at this shit. Damned good. If I didn't want you to know, you would never know. But I need you to know now, and I really need help."

As far as binging went, the years had not dampened any of my skills. This episode was methodical, carefully planned, anticipated, enjoyed, deeply hidden, and devastatingly successful. I was thrilled to be doing it. Mortified when I was in the midst of it. Sad, broken and totally beaten down after the first bite. It was day four when I reached for help. I quickly got the support I needed. I was reminded that I am loved. I was also harshly reminded that binging is a cunning foe, one that demands that I keep working to learn and understand. I almost immediately got into therapy and was finally and officially diagnosed with BED and started getting the help I needed.

So, what was the binge? It was trail mix. Freaking Costco trail mix. I bought four bags. Each weighed four pounds. I paid cash. I ate a bag a day for four days. I ate it all day long. Quietly. One bag at a time. I kept it hidden away and portioned out, so no one would suspect or question or figure out what I was doing.

Your mind is trying to do the math. I'll save you the effort. Each bag contained 36 servings and 9,600 calories. Over four days, I consumed 38,400 calories and 3,360 grams of carbohydrates. My normal daily consumption, by contrast, is about 1,500 calories, with a limit of 90 carbs per day. So ... yeah. The scope of this binge was even more horrifying when I committed all the numbers to writing. And I was also eating my regular meals so that no one would catch on to my binge eating. Eating regular meals to hide my binge eating. Absurd.

I was somehow able to stop the binge, even though I still felt totally out of control and sad and frantic. By reaching out, I went totally against all instincts of a binge-eating haze. It was a humiliating phone call to make. I think I sat on the phone crying for a few moments before I could even mumble "Spencer, I need help." And then I began to battle the shame and guilt, the sense of failure that comes on the heels of losing total control over food. I felt isolated, alone, and terrified I would be found out, or that it wouldn't end. Or that all of my hard work to learn to run and lose weight and reverse diabetes would be gone because I could not, or would not, stop eating. This is an "old friend" I would be happy to never, ever see again. I simply must understand that this "friend" may show up again at any time, for the rest of my life.

Three months later, I found myself in a more emotionally stable spot; I was working to face emotions, rather than feeding them. It was a 24/7 project. There were many subsequent days of battling the compulsion and feeling frantic about food. It bubbles all the time, just below the surface. It's messy, not linear, and kind of scary, yet it's going well. Honest. Now that I know what I'm facing, it's easier to fight back.

I will openly admit there have been days of white knuckling it. There have been days of a constantly annoying, low-level struggle around food, and days of a more intense binge compulsion from sunup to sundown. I have had moments of realization and grief, meltdowns and giddy successes. And, whew! An increasing number of days when I really do feel sane and balanced. Some wonderful people have reached out to offer support and encouragement. Many have told me their own stories. I quickly learned I am not alone—even though not many people talk openly about binge eating, and not everyone knows how to help someone in their life who may be struggling with BED.

I made it my goal to determine what triggered this binge-eating episode, so I could avoid a repeat. I reached the conclusion that there was no single thing, that it was the perfect storm of a whole bunch of stuff that unleashed this specific binge. I had hidden BED, pretending fervently that it no longer existed, that it was tightly controlled with rules and habits. And then it was loose. And running wild. It had been there all along, no matter what I thought. I just hit the right set of conditions and it roared back to life.

I had not had a good year with running. With only four races, three were DNFs. I was burnt out on my routine — on running, journaling food, watching the scale, and work stresses. I had some big, exciting life changes that I was working to make happen in my professional life. You know, life. I was convinced I was balancing and managing it quite well. Then suddenly it was the straw that broke this camel's back.

I am learning to appropriately identify and face my emotions as I feed my body and my lifestyle. Any emotion a human can possibly experience, I can mask as "hunger" ... and eat it. I've done this for as long as I can remember. I have decades of experience in acknowledging, then denying or ignoring, an emotion. Happy or sad, it doesn't seem to matter. Inevitably, I decide that eating is the best possible solution for dealing with fear or happiness, anger or joy, sadness or lack of belonging.

Food is a comfort, a problem and an answer, all in one. I'm still in the process of rudely breaking them the hell up. I'm figuring out what emotions are, how to feel them, and how not to feed them. Just the other day, I was standing in front of the fridge. I was opening and closing, opening and closing the door, trying to decide if I were truly hungry. It must have looked as if I were fanning myself with the door.

Am I hungry? *Open fridge door.* Or am I feeling sad? *Close fridge door.* Am I hungry or am I feeling anxious? Am I hungry or did I get my feelings hurt? I really couldn't figure out the answer. I grabbed a glass of water, walked away from the fridge, and sat myself in a time out. I did a quick scan, head to toe, to see if I was feeling the emotions anywhere but in my belly. I had made a pretty big run and was increasing mileage for the week. I thought carefully about the stresses of the day and week, reviewed my food journal, and decided I was really, truly belly-hungry. Ha! All of that thinking and pondering and wondering made me really, truly hungry for some calories. So I ate one portion of something healthy and filling.

A Cornell University study estimates that most "normal" human beings make more than 200 food-related decisions a day! Wow. Go to bed, wake up, start making another 200 decisions. No wonder fighting an eating disorder is exhausting work.

Ultras and Binge Eating Disorder (BED)

Most of the information I find on eating disorders addresses anorexia or bulimia. Yet I cannot find anything specific about the relationship between binge eating disorder and endurance running. Ultras and BED, it seems to me, are inextricably and pretty wickedly connected bedmates. From the first "Holy shit, could this really be what's happening?" moment, to the "Wow! Makes sense, even though I detest the idea," it took me about six months to puzzle it out. My trigger was the acute episode of BED rearing its ugly head along with a planned off-season break from running. Running was no longer there to hide behind, and its absence made my situation brutally and undeniably clear. It ended in a binge of trail mix, ironically enough, for this trail and ultrarunner.

Hiking one day, I was gobsmacked with the realization that I was using running to hide and feed the BED. I couldn't see this nasty, covert, and destructive cycle because I was so deeply in it. I wasn't running from something or to something. I was running for something and it wasn't something good or worthwhile or sustainable. I stopped in my tracks, sat my butt down on the side of the trail, and wrote some notes on my phone as a newt cruised past to see what I was doing. This felt big. Here's what I wrote:

I love long runs and I hate tapering. I run for long periods, five hours or more, and give myself permission to eat anything and everything in the quantities I want. When I taper (cutting back on activity prior to a race - so you are bottling up the energy), my food intake is restricted and my weight creeps up. When I run long and eat how I want, I basically don't get caught bingeing because the huge volume of food I'm eating is "acceptable" in these crazy running circles. Tapering unleashes sneaky-ass behaviors that I thought I'd banished once and for all … including lying about food.

BED brain thinks about food as an acceptable, necessary, or urgent replacement for something missing, or to fill an emotional need. It has nothing to do with hunger, not a single thing. For me, food can take the place of damned near every emotion on the spectrum. I'm just as likely to eat that emotion in the form of trail mix as I am to simply feel and experience it. No amount of cajoling, shaming, or lecturing can fix it. I've often said, "Pizza was never mean to me." When you have that kind of relationship with food, you need professional help. I wasn't running for the love of running. I was very much running to manage my weight, as I binge but don't purge. I was very much running to make the occasional huge volume of post-run food I was consuming not look out of whack.

I was running to hide my eating disorder, even when I didn't know I had an eating disorder.

I decided I was ready to face all of this and not ignore it or hide it any more. I was scared shitless, but I was ready. I needed help beyond caring and concerned friends. After muscling my way through the post-acute phase of intense blues — of shame, depression, anxiety, hopelessness, and panic — that lasts for days after a bingeing episode ... I got into therapy. Within the first 20 minutes of our first session, my brand-new therapist immediately diagnosed that running was an issue. I instantly told her she was dead wrong, and not politely. I was rude and defiant. Defiance is my go-to when I'm ashamed, and when someone is getting close to the reason for my shame or embarrassment. I flat-out denied the connection. I had lost 200 pounds and reversed diabetes. Running had saved me. Who the hell was this woman to say that running was now a problem? Was she not listening to me? The therapist quickly said we could agree to disagree about the role of running in my eating disorder. We would focus on other things (a smart ploy!). That lasted two sessions. I began to honestly assess what I was doing, and why. I began journaling impulses and noting emotions. I started to make tentative connections between my feelings and food. And then it became obvious. Even to me. I'll be damned if she wasn't right.

In writing everything down, it was impossible to ignore the connection. Running sat smack in the middle of the BED pile. About two sessions into my therapy, I had to concede she had a point. More than a point, in fact. Ultrarunning was the 500-pound gorilla in the room. I hadn't replaced food with running. I had used running to hide, enable, and deny my BED. This was a crucial distinction. I had not let go of one thing and grasped tightly onto something new. In fact, I hadn't given up anything at all. I had just masked what in hell was really going on.

I think the college students with whom I worked at the time would call that a hot mess.

For me, ultras and BED are wed to one another, in epically dysfunctional fashion. As long as I ran long, I could pretend that eating 3,000-plus calories after a long run was normal recovery. Eating whatever I wanted for the week of 60 miles of training was acceptable given that I was burning roughly 9,000 calories. I basically kept signing up for races to make sure I still had high-mileage weeks and full training schedules. That meant my bingeing wouldn't be detected because it looked like acceptable calorie replacement for a solid training week. And while the calories might have been balancing out, it was the motive behind needing those mass quantities of food that was the very heart of the issue.

Fuck. I was walking on a greased, loosely tied tightrope.

So what now? Great question.

- Awareness is a huge part of the battle—talking about it openly, knowing that my ultrarunner friends support me when I get "wonky" or weird about food or food discussions.

- My main strategy for staying focused is choosing not to run ultras for a while. I need a break from running. I am using this downtime in all the best ways possible and not viewing it as punishment.

- When the time comes to hit the trails again, I will rebuild my running from the ground up, slowly and carefully. I know that food is fuel, and that's the only place it will hold in my running.

I didn't take on this whole lifestyle change to give up when things got hard.

9 CHAPTER NINE
ADVICE AND BOUNDARIES

One of the most common questions I'm asked about my lifestyle change is this: "How do I talk to someone I love about their need to lose weight?" The basic answer, based upon my personal experience, is that you really should not. You cannot motivate another person to embrace big changes.

Others I've talked to, folks like me who have embarked on significant life change journeys, echo my sentiments. We agree that we were ultimately motivated by some seemingly random moment in time, a collection of small happenings, or a life-altering incident. The decision to make the lasting, hard changes was never spurred on by someone's "helpful comments." In fact, the opposite seems to be true. On those occasions when people tried to talk to us about our weight or health, we weren't ready to listen. We were resentful and defensive to the message bearer for what we saw as a personal attack on our weight and eating habits. That's not exactly a great setup, or fertile ground, for healthy conversations (or conversions).

Nothing that anyone said to me about my weight or my diabetes ever convinced me to change for the long term. None of it—subtle, friendly, mean, direct, scientific, joking—it didn't matter. When someone approached me about my weight or health, or how my body looked, I'd make short-term and panicked changes out of grief or embarrassment or even blind hope. I wasn't ready to do the wholesale, gritty work needed to make a sustainable change. No one could have convinced, guilted, cajoled, or begged me into doing it until I was ready.

- Grocery shopping at 350-plus pounds, I was embarking on yet another diet I'd found in some magazine, or had been told about by a friend who was easily and miraculously shedding weight. I was loading up my cart for a successful start to a new diet. I had "light" everything, including ice cream. Everything in the cart was on the plan. A skinny, older man stopped me in the pasta aisle, looked me squarely in the eye after inspecting my cart, and said loudly, "You really don't need all that ice cream and junk food." I left the full cart in the middle of the aisle and went straight home, totally mortified.

- I had an aunt ask me, "You don't think drinking diet soda will make you thin, do you?" I was about thirteen at the time. I remember thinking that I did, in fact, believe diet soda was one of the answers that was going to save me. I mean, it wasn't sugar soda, and Weight Watchers had said it was okay.

- Another relative gave me this ultimatum: "We care about you. You're killing yourself. If you don't change, you won't be around to see your nephews grow up."

- I had multiple friends tell me, in a variety of ways, that the reason I was single was that guys don't date "fat chicks." If I could just lose weight, I could found find that elusive happiness with the right guy.

And these comments were never-ending: "Do you really need to eat that?" "Should you be eating that?" "Aren't you on a diet?" These comments and interactions may have been meant to inspire, enlighten, encourage, scare, or spur me into action, but they were by and large (pun intended!) destructive and hurtful, no matter how the message was delivered or who said it.

When you're fat, unhealthy, overweight, out of shape ... You don't need someone confirming that. You already know it, in all its painful and degrading glory. The statement doesn't make you go, "Wow. Geez. I didn't know that. I should do something about it. I am so glad they said something." No, it wounds you. It pisses you off. It makes you feel deeply ashamed. It beats you down because you know you've tried so, so many things before, and failed. You really, truly do not know what else to do. You're humiliated. You can't hide the problem of being overweight or obese. Hell, you publicly wear your problem for the whole world to see, every minute of every day.

In no way did anyone's "helpful" comments ever give me the power and energy to go to work on the changes that I ultimately would have to make. Fat chance. It may be brutal to say, but you can't help those who are not ready to help themselves. From everything I've read about the paradigm of change, telling someone they have a problem doesn't usually help them move into action to resolve it. The trigger for real, lasting change usually comes from a seemingly innocuous yet life-defining moment. It could be a health scare, a turning of the years, or some other very personal "bottom moment."

The moment in which inspiration for change strikes, and sticks, is very personal and pretty darn hard to explain. For you who continue to insist that someone in your life really needs to make a change, lose weight, and get healthy, I have some suggestions. I understand that you care deeply, are afraid for their health, and you genuinely want to help. You need to do *something*.

When I was truly ready to do the work and make a change in my own life, I sought out people—very special people—as my support team. These are things they have, slowly and quietly, done over the years to help get me to a healthier place. Their actions speak louder than words ever will:

- Listen. Listen for open doors, pleas for help, blatant defensiveness, or fear. Only when they open the door and invite you in do you have permission to engage in a conversation about how you can help. Don't answer questions that have not been asked. Don't offer advice that has not been solicited.

- Set an example. Sign up for a 5K and invite them to join you while you train, either walking or running. Move your normal meeting spots to a walk or coffee shop instead of a bakery or fast-food lunch. Find subtle, genuine ways to shift the patterns of your friendship away from food, and toward conversation and activity.

- Be ready to embrace their change without judgment. There are all kinds of programs that people lean on, cling to, or buy into when they commit to lose weight and change their lifestyle. We may or may not agree with, or even understand, these programs and options. But if someone wants to lose weight, learn new eating habits, and get moving, get out of their way! If someone is simply jazzed that they found something to be excited about, be excited with them! If they're willing to own it, work it, and make it a part of their life, who are we to judge? Our job is to unequivocally support them.

You can lead a horse to water, but you can't make it drink. The horse will drink when it's good and thirsty, not when you think it should be thirsty.

Lighting the Fire

I had a conversation the other day that helped me reignite a fire, one that I had forgotten. And I had to screw up and self-correct to get to the right spot. Here's what happened. I met with a woman I don't know very well. She reached out to me because she had just been given a type 2 diabetes diagnosis. She had more than 100 pounds to lose, and she didn't know where to start. She asked me to tell her how I lost weight and reversed my diabetes. She said she wanted to hear my story.

I tried to find the right words to relate some things about my journey that I thought might be helpful to her. I told her my journey was not linear. It was not easy. Nor was it over. The trade-offs were life-changing in every possible, positive way imaginable. I told her I remembered the day when I mentally understood that I was trading medicine, prescribed in a pill bottle and administered with a syringe, for medicine in the form of healthy, nutrient-dense foods. I remembered when I finally understood that I was trading a lifetime of being lazy, inactive, and comfortable for a new lease on a life that would be wildly uncomfortable, have me running in the woods and facing exhilarating fears head-on. I understood I was in the lifelong process of building an entirely new lifestyle. I wanted her to understand that, with every fiber of my being, I had been willing to trade certain death by diabetes for a chance at what I knew could be a life worth living—loudly, fiercely, and completely—every day.

As I spoke, I had an intense energy building inside of me, in my head and chest. I so wanted her to understand my journey. Yet I could see that I was failing. I felt like she was overwhelmed with the idea that, in her own hands, she had the power to save her own life. Then it finally registered through my thick skull what I was seeing, feeling, and experiencing with her: my story, combined with the image of her own journey stretching ahead, was scaring her. A lot.

Beyond the tears, beyond the averted eyes and bowed head, there was fear. I could see it. She was trying hard to hide it, but it was too big, too pervasive, too consuming. I had to stop and regroup ... for both of us. I stopped, mid-sentence, sat up straight, made solid eye contact and took a few deep breaths. Deep, loud, intentional breaths. This habit has become soothing for me in times of distress. When my friend Wendie breathes that way, she can calm everyone around her, an entire room of people. I have seen it happen. I was trying to steal just a bit of her magic. I was also hoping it would work to help me figure out how to put this conversation back on the right track.

And then I did something that's really hard for me to do: I shut the hell up. And I began to listen to the silence. It was very tense and full. So I just kept breathing. I tried to convey to my companion, simply with my breathing and my eyes, that I could — and would — wait for her, with her, in the fear and uncertainty. I would willingly sit there, ready to listen, and just be with her for as long as she needed me to be there. I wanted her to know that struggling with emotions and words was okay. It was safe, and warranted, and healthy between us. Then I waited for her to fill the silence. Eventually she did. I let her talk, cry, and grapple for words.

That is what I should have done from the very beginning.

See, I have a fire burning in my heart and soul. I want everyone to catch the passion to change what's broken in their lives. To be fired up and excited by the challenges in front of them. Fundamentally, I understand that it has to be their own fire. I can't light it, I can't tend it, and I have no right to even share the flame. This conversation was a perfect reminder for me. Spencer, as my coach, is always reminding me to respect, trust, and work the process. It turned out I really needed the reminder to respect that process for others. It is not my process, not my fire, not my opportunity. It is theirs. This was also a great reminder that I wasn't always fired up and ready to take on the world. I sat there staring at my companion and could suddenly remember when it was me who was terrified, ashamed, and overwhelmed. I could see myself sitting across the table. I remembered when I just wanted someone to listen and understand. When I wanted to be heard by someone who would not judge me, and who maybe would say something I'd never heard before that led me to believe this just might be possible.

I was there, in a similar fireless pit, for a very long time. Too long. And while I thought I wanted someone to light the fire for me, I really just needed someone to listen and understand. Just like when Jennifer listened, pen poised over a napkin, to help me make sense of my goals. When that happened? That is when things finally caught fire for me. I want to be the person for others that I so desperately needed when I began this journey. This conversation reminded me that people don't need to hear my story, they need me to care about theirs.

Setting Boundaries

Having just said people need me to care about their stories … there's a flip side to this as well. And it took me a while to figure it out.

One of the most challenging pieces of my lifestyle change journey has been learning about boundaries. Some I had to learn, some I have set, and some I'm just now stumbling into. It usually stems from something quasi-related to caring about others' lives and stories; it's when they want me to solve their problems, do their work, or they simply need to say out loud why they're not ready to do the hard work and they want someone to agree with them. It's exhausting. It took me a long while to discern when someone was really ready to be honest about what changes they needed to make and were ready to be held accountable. I was shocked at how many wanted a magic bullet or an excuse or, well, anything other than actually doing the work needed to make the changes.

Once I got my hands on some of the science behind behavior change, this all made a whole lot more sense. I knew that what I had done was against a whole lot of odds. The statistics put into perspective why I was having so many "save me" conversations as opposed to the rare "help me figure out how to do this on my own" conversations. They say one in 124 obese women have the chance of getting to a "normal" weight. I'm almost always willing to be in fairly intimate conversations with people (even strangers!) who want advice or a listening ear, or who want to share their struggles and successes. I speak publicly, openly, and honestly about my own journey, what I've learned and the changes I've made in my life. I understand that this might seem a conflicting sort of confession.

As I've never considered myself to be a guarded person, establishing these needed boundaries has been new and uncomfortable ground for me. At first, not fully understanding what was going on, I did what I usually do at first when things get difficult: I ignored it all. That's a genetic trait, I'm pretty sure. Big, scary, hard topics, coupled with my deeply embedded worry that I might disappoint or hurt someone—I just averted my eyes and hoped it would all just go away. Even when it was painfully obvious that ignoring some of these growing issues was not a healthy or sustainable strategy, I continued to fight against setting boundaries. It just felt wrong and selfish.

I was two years into my journey when I finally connected with a handful of individuals via social media who had "walked in my shoes" and truly understood what I was trying to do. They'd been there, done that. It was so exciting to finally make these connections! Over time, in our conversations, each of them has expressed roughly the same version of sentiments about our respective journeys: It is a lonely, hard, life-changing, I-will-never-go-back, you-really-have-to-do-it-on-your-own, kind of road. The other common angst that emerged from our conversations was just because we lost more than a 100 pounds, and reversed diabetes, did not mean we were ready or able to help someone else with their journey ... no matter how badly we wanted to help, nor how much others wanted us to help them. Sometimes we just can't be there for someone else. They have issues that trigger things in us, we need to focus on our own health, or they're too needy and that's not something we have the emotional energy for at that time in our own journey. I started to understand why it took me so long to find this small handful of people who are successful and also carefully guarding that success. I started to understand where all my conflicting emotions were coming from as well.

I saw my inability to handle the pressure of helping others as a serious character flaw. They helped me begin to see it for what it was — just another part of the process. Another skill to learn. I was routinely overwhelmed by the fact that, even though I'd been on this journey, I couldn't answer all the questions from others. I couldn't help everyone find, or stay on, their own path, and I couldn't provide full emotional support to others on their own journeys. I'm just one person who's still trying to figure out her own life. "Bets," Jeff asked, "have you thought of the fact that you could drown while trying to help someone else?" I mean, I know I was put on this planet to help people. Yet this is a basic truth: If I'm not actively focused and actively working on my own health and wholeness and stability, what good can I possibly do for anyone else?

10 CHAPTER TEN
A NEW REALITY

You've heard a lot about Spencer, but there's something important you might not know about him at this point. Beyond being my business partner, coach, and one of my best friends, he's also a recovering alcoholic and addict, more than five years sober.

He started coaching me while he was teetering on the apex of heading toward the bottom. The bottom that he would thankfully survive and would lead to his sobriety. I spent about six months being coached by an active drunk and had no clue he was drinking or struggling. Not a single clue. I remember with absolute clarity the day he texted me in February of 2014 saying "Need to meet with you now." He sat with me and told me that he was a drunk and an addict and was one day sober. "If you want to get a new coach and cut me out of your life, I'll totally understand. I'll help you find a new coach." I replied with "I am not going anywhere. What can I do to help you?" And I meant it with every fiber of my being. I wasn't going anywhere. He'd been there for me through losing more weight, figuring out compression so my belly flap of skin wouldn't beat me to death when running, taking my phone calls when someone had said something unkind and I was emotionally unraveling and battling shame. He'd been there for me. I was going to be there for him.

As he built up days and months of sobriety, we would have great conversations about the heartbreak of friends ghosting us, not driving by the haunts that tempted us for food or drink, the difficulty of staying open and engaged with our accountability systems. We would talk a lot about taking it one single day at a time. Suddenly my coach was also becoming my friend and we were talking honestly and openly about the hard crap that is involved with this type of journey. And we began to slowly realize that regardless of why we had each hit a bottom, the climb out had a whole lot of similarities. Then one day he went public with his struggles. Alcoholics don't often do that. Recovery programs often encourage anonymity for a reason, but he was tired of hiding and tired of not living his life the way he wanted to live it.

Need to come clean about something. Earlier this year, in February, a rare snowstorm hit Corvallis (Oregon) and pretty much shut the city down. That weekend I had planned a three-day training block on my bike, but because of snow, I was unable to get out and the last thing I was going to do was spend three hours on a trainer. Instead of training, I hunkered down for three days and drank, a lot, by myself. It turned out to be the straw that broke the camel's back. That Monday morning, I woke up hungover, depressed, emotionally depleted, and decided that it was finally time to address my issues with addiction, 100 percent…no more half-assing it. Attempting sobriety had been a long time coming.

I began ramping up my alcoholic/addictive tendencies in 2006 when my life was firmly out of control financially, emotionally, and professionally. My addiction then, among other things, was Ninkasi Tricerahops Double IPA and Crown Royal. I snuck it most evenings, and sometimes mornings, for two years, unbeknownst to most, even in my inner circle. Fast forward nine years later and I had become a professional closet drinker. Add in the fact that I was training my ass off for various running and road bike races, I actually took pride knowing that I could spend an entire Friday evening partying, to wake up on Saturday and bust out a four-hour run.

I remember telling myself that I'm unique, I can party this hard and train at a high level, look at me, look at me. Well, this turned out to be complete bullshit and was ultimately part of the behavior that led to my sober date, 2/11/14. I'm still very new to sobriety and in no way am I an expert on the subject … and I will never pretend to be. So far, it's been a very humbling experience, and very scary at times. I've got a tremendous support system of friends and family and I am very thankful for this. Rather than obsessing on the future and what will happen five years from now, I think I'm just going to try and enjoy the fact that today, it's sunny in Corvallis, and there are some trails calling my name.

The outpouring of support from that public confession blew his mind. Replies on the post, texts, calls, emails. His world was suddenly filled with encouragement and love from near and far, those close to him as well as those he only knew from social media. It was *all* positive. He will tell you sobriety was one of the best decisions he's made and he's grateful. And he's living a life he only dreamed of while he was drunk.

Spencer, solo run in the Mac Forest to celebrate his sober anniversary.

He's a published author who wrote *Appetite for Addiction* and business co-owner of Novo Veritas. One of his childhood dreams was to be an athlete. He's now actively chasing down that childhood dream, training full time as a triathlete; and it's only possible because he focuses as intently on his training as he does his sobriety.

He takes each day as it comes. One day at a time.

Novo Veritas

My business venture with Spencer, Novo Veritas, is off and running (pun totally intended), and four years old. Our mission is to inspire, empower, and provide accountability to people to embrace the pursuit of change. And our business format reflects that. It's pretty simple and falls into two parts: coaching people chasing down big lifestyle changes, and speaking to others about our stories.

People come to us for coaching because they are or have been 100-plus pounds overweight, they want to be or are in recovery, and/or they are facing a medical diagnosis that needs lifestyle changes and they have no idea where to start. And oftentimes, they don't have a support system to help them get started. We are trying to be the people we needed when we were in the throes of these changes. We've been in their shoes and we've gotten personal training as well as health-and-wellness coaching certifications, well beyond our own experiences, to try to help others find stable footing and a new path.

We are invited to present in a variety of settings, to all kinds of audiences. Our entire aim is to connect with those who need to know they're not alone. We keep our presentations more conversational than formal. We talk bluntly and honestly about our lifestyle changes and the crap that led us each to make an overhaul of our lives. We purposely save half of our time for the audience to ask us questions. Any questions. They can, and do, ask us anything. Things get authentic and candid very quickly. Spencer and I do not shy away from talking about the painful and ugly stuff. We try to address how each of us got to the point of being ready for major change, and how we made those changes. We discuss what our respective journeys look like today. And we keep that space safe for everyone involved so they feel free to ask us the questions that perhaps they've never uttered aloud.

And our main message with our entire business? You'll hear this in our presentations and it's also ingrained in our coaching format. There is no magic bullet. Changing your lifestyle is hard. No shortcuts, no magic, nothing instant.

- Get honest with yourself and acknowledge there's a problem.

- Identify the obstacles.

- Make a plan.

- Work your butt off every single day.

Repeat. Repeat again. And again.

One of our first public presentations as Novo Veritas.

After one recent presentation, we had a conversation with our friend Patrick Means. It was the kind of conversation that doesn't need to be very long to make one really start thinking. Patrick is a thoughtful guy, one hell of a talented cyclist, a photographer, and a storyteller. In the short time I have known him, I discovered that he uses words very intentionally, and he won't back away from hard or uncomfortable topics. Patrick said that what Spencer and I had talked about was a solid reminder that everyone around us is battling something hard and scary. We may never know what it is that someone is fighting, or even if they are winning or losing, but we cannot give up on people. Ever. Even when they want to give up on themselves.

That conversation with Patrick got me thinking about the random kindnesses that have been shown to me during this lifestyle journey. The times when people didn't give up on me, when they threw kindness in my direction even when I wanted to give up on myself. It was easy for me to see the application of Patrick's words in my own life. So easy. These are a few of the random kind moments that made a difference, and have stuck with me:

The woman (and her little wiggly-butted dog) on Bald Hill who always said a very cheery "Good morning" and waved at me during my walks and halting runs in the spring of 2013. Every time. Maybe even a 100 times.

The five-year-old girl at the Denver airport who curiously watched me testing my blood with a finger stick. She wandered over when I caught her watching and smiled at her to make sure she wasn't scared of my medical testing equipment. She told me her grandma had "the sugar disease," too. She sat there knowingly, waiting for my meter to beep, then asked my number. When I reported double (not triple) digits, she patted my arm and told me, "Good job."

The skinny, lightning-fast dude with the late start at the Corvallis Half Marathon in 2012 who sprinted past me around mile eight, as I was walking just as fast as I could, and yelled, "Girl! You've totally got this!"

The college-age guy at the gym who came over to respectfully and tentatively express concern that I would hurt my shoulder because of my weight-lifting form. He offered to show me the right way to hold the weights. He was smiling and non-threatening and was sincere in trying to help me.

The baristas at the local coffee drive-through who leaned out the window and told me they could tell I was losing weight and without meaning to be creepy, could they please tell me that I looked healthy and happy, and they were proud of me?

These acts of kindness were pure, happy, and cost nothing for the person giving. Friend or stranger, it didn't matter. They came at a time when I needed that support, and they had no way of knowing that. It cost them nothing and meant everything. Everyone is battling something and these are simple reminders of what kindness can look like in our world. These are the reasons we started this business. These are the reasons that keep us sharing our stories and working with people who simply need someone to believe in them and their crazy goals and dreams.

Why I Coach

"These mountains that you are carrying, you were only supposed to climb."
— *Najwa Zebian*

This is my favorite quote. These words often worm their way into my mind during a tough workout or race as a sort of mantra. If you were running/cycling with me you might hear me mumbling "… climb …" Sometimes with an expletive. Sometimes just that single word. For a long while, this was a mind-expanding epiphany. Now it's profoundly motivating and a touchstone of sorts. This quote has found its way to the core of my coaching philosophy.

Turns out I was not the only one trying to freaking carry the Cascade Mountain Range on my back when it was meant to be climbed, explored, enjoyed. When someone is tackling a lifestyle shift that involves triple-digit weight loss, or battling health complications that accompany obesity, or reversing life-long unhealthy behaviors, there's some… uh… tremendous baggage we have to trip over, name, claim, move, throw away, and figure out along the way. Mountains of shit. Mountains.

So, I have one simple job at the very start: I listen to their mountain(s). Listen patiently and with grace, creating space for them to be raw, honest, and share things they've perhaps never said aloud, confessed, or acknowledged to another person. When someone is willing to trust you and tell you how they got to a place they really don't want to stay, a place that might even be trying to kill them, a place they don't remember arriving at … A place that is oddly and sadly more comforting than the unknown of trying to change … Honor them by listening to them talk about the mountains they are carrying. They're going to have to learn in their own way, and in their own time, that those mountains were meant to be climbed.

If I'm really lucky, they'll invite me along for the learning, work, sweat, and adventure that follows when they learn to climb their mountain one step at a time. I get asked "Why do you coach?" and "What kind of people do you coach?" The simple truth? I got certified as a health and wellness coach because I wanted to be the person I needed when I was losing weight, reversing diabetes, and learning to be active as a morbidly obese woman. I'm coaching the kind of people I was just a few short years ago. I was obese, morbidly obese, grossly overweight, fat. Call it what you want. I was very ill, unhealthy, with a lifestyle-induced disease. Yet I had this wild, burning desire to change things and *not a single clue* where to start. I needed help.

There were a whole lot of wonderful/helpful/supportive humans who had (and still have) my back, and I refuse to deny their role in helping me change my life. The other truth is that I needed a level of specialized expertise I couldn't find. You can't take someone who is inactive and carrying 100 to 300-plus extra pounds and apply a normal weight-loss and activity plan. You can't. Well you can, and the desperate client is going to try to do what's being asked, and they're likely going to get hurt and discouraged and give up. I know what I'm talking about. That cycle of failure is one I know intimately.

The coach has two jobs. First, believe in your client. Second, start from where they are, not where they used to be, or where they think they should be.

- What do you do if you can't reach your feet to tie your shoes? Or normal shoes don't fit on your feet?

- Where can you find a 48F bra that you can actually run in? How do you compress belly rolls or other body bulk so you don't get hurt when trying to move?

- What if you're terrified that you'll get laughed at, or the race times won't allow you to be on the course because you're slow, or the gym equipment won't be rated for your weight?

- How do you start running/moving when you weigh 300-plus pounds?

- What if you have complicating medical conditions that limit what you do? We're not talking handy excuses, but real physical barriers.

- What if no one else in your life supports your desire or efforts to change?

- What if you can't do even day one of the Couch to 5K program? You can't even get on the gym floor to try a sit-up or push-up? You get winded walking up the stairs to the indoor track?

The issues that the obese face and deal with in their daily lives can swamp them before they even get started on a routine. They see the mountain they have to carry or climb; *when you're 100-plus pounds overweight, "carry" and "climb" seem to be the same effing insurmountable level of effort needed.* They know it's going to be messy, uncomfortable, lonely, discouraging, and hard and they barely have the energy to get through the day. They've likely failed in previous attempts. They need someone who's been there and can help them navigate the barriers and feel some hope and stay focused on the long-term goals.

I have a health-and-wellness coaching certification with the American Council on Exercise. This past fall I went one step further and got additional education and training in working with those who are inactive, obese, and/or are dealing with chronic illnesses. I spent hours learning how to get people moving safely and get some solid lifestyle skills in place to keep them moving toward health. It was odd to learn about all of this and look back and apply it to my own journey. I got a lot right with sheer determination and dumb luck. I got plenty of stuff wrong – and now I know better and will help others do better.

As someone invited into a life-changing process, how can I help people learn to climb the mountain instead of carrying it?

I coach because I have been in their shoes. And their 48F bra. And their sweat-drenched clothes from walking a mile. I have warily eyed a piece of gym equipment and wondered if it could handle my weight. I coach because I love helping people find a new, healthy path in their life. I coach because the people I'm lucky enough to support are doing the exceptionally hard work of trying to get a handle on their lives. I know, as their coach, that I'm being invited into a special place in their journey — to help them figure out how to get started climbing when they're standing at the bottom of a mountain and aiming for the top.

BACK ON THE MOUNTAIN

I often reflect back on that moment on the mountain ridge in Colorado. That moment when it finally hit me with full force: *this is my life*. The days of wondering, from the safety of my (extended seat belt) airline seat, what it would be like to see those mountains up close are over. The journey since that moment has taken me to even higher summits and right back down to the valley floor a time or two.

The path for me was not straight, consistent or even clearly marked, and it won't be for you either. There will be false summits, storms will roll in, you'll lose the trail, or you'll simply find yourself in a really deep valley and wonder where in the hell you are and how you even got there.

Or maybe that's where you are right now. Don't quit; rest. Sit your butt down on a fallen log and figure out what you need to do to keep going forward. One step at a time. That's all. Then stand up, brush off your butt and start putting one foot in front of the other again, because quitting won't get you where you really want to go.

There are mountains to climb.

ACKNOWLEDGEMENTS

'The effects of kindness are not always seen immediately. Sometimes it takes years until your kindness will pay off, and its returned to you. And sometimes you never see the fruits of your labors, but they are there, deep inside of the soul of the one you touched.' – *Dan Kelly*

Finding the heart-deep words to say thank you was way, way harder than getting out of a sweaty sports bra. It was easily the hardest part of writing this book. There are so many people who are indelible and important parts of the adventure, who have heaped kindness on me, and who walked beside me. My heart and soul wear their fingerprints.

Joey and **Justin Johnson**. You're two of the main reasons that I fought so hard to change my life. I wanted to be alive to watch you both grow and thrive. The thing in life that I cherish the most is being your aunt.

Mom and **Dad**. I knew you were proud of me and loved me each and every single day. You raised your daughters to be strong and self-reliant. And Dad, I am convinced that the stubborn grit that serves me so well in the tough stuff is straight from your side of the gene pool. Mom, you were my best friend, your death shattered my heart into a million little pieces and I still miss you every single day.

Deb and **Dan Johnson**. Supporting crazy food ideas, showing up at finish lines, and reminding me to not let life limit me. You two have kept me safe in some of the rough and scary moments of discovering my new life, without allowing me to stay stuck there.

Spencer Newell. I thought I'd stumbled into a coach who would simply help me learn how to run. I had no idea that our chance encounter would morph into you becoming one of my best friends, my business partner, and that you would still be my coach six years later. You believed in me when I couldn't fathom believing in myself. That gift made all the difference in this journey.

Josh and **Wendie Gum**. Thank you for your support, encouragement, and an appropriate pinch of get-it-done, all in the right moments and usually with a ton of humor. We have spent hours running together, getting epically lost in more than a few forests, fixing life's problems, and learning new life skills. "I have this really crazy idea, just hear me out…"

Wade Foster. Breathe and poop. You always remind me that one of these two things is likely to solve most of the problems we're going to encounter in life. You were there at the very first shaky steps of me trying to figure this whole thing out, and you haven't left my side.

Jeff Sherman. Teaching me how to blow a snot rocket and how to use online dating apps. Getting talked into any adventure even before you have all the details. Buying me a pocket knife and bear spray so I would be safe while running. And not losing your cool when we were running and needed the knife to cut my hair loose from a bramble bush and the knife was stowed very carefully away in the back of my running vest and totally out of reach.

Anneke Tucker Griffith. I remember one of the first times you came to work out with me. We were going to climb stairs. I was stalling for all I was worth trying to try to get out of it. You just smiled and sat back in the chair and said, "Oh. I'll wait for you. No problem." And you did. And we eventually went and climbed stairs and I cussed you the entire time. And then we did that weekly for several months. Thank you for being so strong, loving and stubborn.

Hannah O'Leary. We were walking partners long before any of this began. You were there for the very first race and helped me pin my race bib on when my hands were shaking. You damn near threw your body onto the hood of the volunteer cop car trying to close the course behind me, after you gave him a piece of your mind, all to allow me to finish the race. We solved the world's problems, took a ton of pictures, and saved a whole hell of a lot of worms on our walks. My heart has your fingerprints all over it.

Jennifer Viña. Lunch and planning out life on a napkin. Nothing but support when the dreams were big and the risks seemed absurd. You were there at the pivotal moment when I felt hope take hold. I remember the hug and the unconditional support as I took those very first steps with you right by my side.

Nick Fleury and **Michael Murphey**. *me, whispering with panicked wide-eyes* "Nick, he just said to grab dumbbells ... which ones are those...?" Oh the joy I had in learning to lift weights with an incredible teacher, Murphey, and an accidental pairing with my long-term weights partner, Nick. You two allowed me to learn and get strong and feel comfortable with something that was wholly new to me.

Scott Reed. I have to wonder how different things would be if you, now the retired Oregon State University Vice-Provost for Outreach and Engagement, had not stopped Spencer and I one day to tell us that we should really find a way to help other people with our stories and life experiences. Your encouragement led to the development of Novo Veritas.

Anne Miller, Rita VanDoren, Bonnie Wright, and **Erica McKenzie**. I have spent more time getting lost on trails, learning running, solving life's problems, and savoring trail time with the four of you than just about anyone. Each and every single time my feet hit the trail, I give thanks for your friendships and that you each have allowed me into your lives.

Trail, Ultrarunning Community. If we shared time on the trail, got lost, raced/crewed/volunteered together, previewed a course, found a new trail, guarded each other while peeing/pooping on the trail, dragged each other along on a hard workout, picked each other up off the ground, waited for race lottery results... You are part of the reason I feel so welcomed in this amazing community.

Patrick Means. You captured the perfect headshot for this book and countless other random snapshots with your exquisite eye for storytelling. **Joanna Larsen.** You designed the Novo Veritas logo five years ago and then took my rough ideas for a book cover and made magic. **Sharon Ezzeldin.** Thank you for managing my frustration with the writing process and guiding me to organize and create new stories to make my blog into a book. **John Gottberg**. I can't say how much I appreciate your help with writing this book.

Dr. Mark Cucuzzella. Professor of Family Medicine at West Virginia University. We connected in the ultrarunning world and I quickly learned you knew a whole lot about type 2 diabetes. You provided some technical assistance for this book as well as answering a handful of really odd diabetes/ultrarunning questions along the way.

Raven Eye Photography, Todd Weselake. You captured so many amazing shots during TransRockies 2016 for so many runners, but the cover shot is one of my favorites. Thank you for letting me use your art in (and on) my book.

Kerri Chavez. Our friendship picks up where it left off and then just keeps getting better. We keep meandering down paths others would easily pass by or ignore.

Heartfelt gratitude for so many people, not mentioned by name, who have been part of this journey. I know who you are. I proudly wear your fingerprints on my soul.

'She was a girl with a mountain to climb.' - Markus Zusak

RESOURCES AND ADDITIONAL INFORMATION

Find Novo Veritas online at www.novo-veritas.com, and on Facebook and Instagram.

Email queries may be directed to **Novo.Veritas@gmail.com**.

Read Betsy's blog at <u>allbetsareoff392.wordpress.com</u>.

Printed in Poland
by Amazon Fulfillment
Poland Sp. z o.o., Wrocław

32112571R00106